Table Of Contents

INTRODUCTION

The Salter Air fryer is an easy way to cook delicious healthy meals. Rather than cooking the food in oil and hot fat that may affect your health, the machine uses rapid hot air to circulate around and cook meals. This allows the outside of your food to be crispy and ensures that the inside layers are cooked through.

The Salter Air fryer allows us to cook almost everything and a lot of dishes. We can use the Salter Air fryer for cooking Meat, vegetables, poultry, fruit, fish, and a wide variety of desserts. It is possible to prepare your entire meals, starting from appetizers to main courses and desserts. Not to mention, The Salter Air fryer also allows homemade preserves or even delicious sweets and cakes.

How Does the Salter Air fryer Works?

The technology of the Salter Air fryer is very simple. Fried foods get their crunchy texture because hot oil heats foods quickly and evenly on their surface. Oil is an excellent heat conductor, which helps with fast and simultaneous cooking across all ingredients. For decades cooks have used convection ovens to mimic the effects of frying or cooking the whole surface of the food. But the air never circulates quickly enough to achieve that delicious surface crisp we all love in fried foods.

With this mechanism, the air is circulated on high degrees, up to 200° C, to "air fry" any food such as fish, chicken or chips, etc. This technology has changed the whole idea of cooking by reducing the fat up to 80% compared to old-fashioned deep fat frying.

The Salter Air fryer cooking releases the heat through a heating element that cooks the food more healthily and appropriately. There's also an exhaust fan right above the cooking chamber, which provides the food required airflow. This way, food is cooked with constant heated air. This leads to the same heating temperature reaching every single part of the food that is being cooked. So, this is an only grill and the exhaust fan that is helping the Salter Air fryer to boost air at a constantly high speed to cook healthy food with less fat.

The internal pressure increases the temperature that will then be controlled by the exhaust system. Exhaust fan also releases extra filtered air to cook the food in a much healthier way. The Salter Air fryer has no odor at all, and it is absolutely harmless, making it user and environment-friendly.

Benefits of the Salter Air Fryer:

- Healthier, oil-free meals
- It eliminates cooking odors through internal air filters
- Makes cleaning easier due to lack of oil grease
- The Salter Air Fryer can bake, grill, roast and fry providing more options
- A safer method of cooking compared to deep frying with exposed hot oil
- Has the ability to set and leave, as most models and it includes a digital timer

The Salter Air fryer is an all-in-one that allows cooking to be easy and quick. It also leads to a lot of possibilities once you get to know it. Once you learn the basics and become familiar with your Salter Air fryer, you can feel free to experiment and modify the recipes in the way you prefer. You can prepare a vast number of dishes in the Salter Air fryer, and you can adapt your favorite stove-top dish, so it becomes air fryer–friendly. It all boils down to variety and lots of options, right?

Cooking perfect and delicious as well as healthy meals has never been easier. You can see how this recipe collection proves itself.

Enjoy!

Breakfast

Air Fryer Hard-Boiled Eggs
PREP: 1 MINUTE • COOK TIME: 15 MINUTES • TOTAL: 16 MINUTES• SERVES: 6

Ingredients
6 eggs

Instructions
1   Place the eggs in the air fryer basket. (You can put the eggs in an oven-safe bowl if you are worried about them rolling around and breaking.)
2   Set the temperature of your Salter AF to 250°F. Set the timer and bake for 15 minutes (if you prefer a soft-boiled egg, reduce the cook time to 10 minutes). Meanwhile, fill a medium mixing bowl half full of ice water. Use tongs to remove the eggs from the air fryer basket, and transfer them to the ice water bath. Let the eggs sit for 5 minutes in the ice water.
    Peel and eat on the spot or refrigerate for up to 1 week.
Per Serving: Calories: 72; Fat: 5g; Saturated fat: 2g; Carbohydrate: 0g; Fiber: 0g; Sugar: 0g; Protein: 6g; Iron: 1mg; Sodium: 70mg

Easy Air Fryer Baked Eggs with Cheese
PREP: 2 MINUTES • COOK TIME: 6 MINUTES • TOTAL: 8 MINUTES •SERVES: 2

Ingredients
2 large eggs
2 tablespoons half-and-half, divided
2 teaspoons shredded Cheddar cheese, divided

Salt
Freshly ground black pepper

Instructions
1   Lightly coat the insides of 2 (8-ounce) ramekins with cooking spray. Break an egg into each ramekin. Add 1 tablespoon of half-and-half and 1 teaspoon of cheese to each ramekin. Season with salt and pepper. Using a fork, stir the egg mixture. Set the ramekins in the air fryer basket.
2   Set the temperature of your Salter AF to 330°F. Set the timer and bake for 6 minutes. Check the eggs to make sure they are cooked. If they are not done, cook for 1 minute more and check again.

Bacon-and-Eggs Avocado

PREP: 5 MINUTES • COOK TIME: 17 MINUTES • TOTAL: 22 MINUTES • SERVES: 1

Ingredients

1 large egg
1 avocado, halved, peeled, and pitted
2 slices bacon

Fresh parsley, for serving (optional)
Sea salt flakes, for garnish (optional)

Instructions

1. Spray the Salter air fryer basket with avocado oil. Preheat the Salter air fryer to 320°F. Fill a small bowl with cool water.

2. Soft-boil the egg: Place the egg in the air fryer basket. Cook for 6 minutes for a soft yolk or 7 minutes for a cooked yolk. Transfer the egg to the bowl of cool water and let sit for 2 minutes. Peel and set aside. Use a spoon to carve out extra space in the center of the avocado halves until the cavities are big enough to fit the soft-boiled egg. Place the soft-boiled egg in the center of one half of the avocado and replace the other half of the avocado on top, so the avocado appears whole on the outside.

   Starting at one end of the avocado, wrap the bacon around the avocado to completely cover it. Use toothpicks to hold the bacon in place. Place the bacon-wrapped avocado in the Salter air fryer basket and cook for 5 minutes. Flip the avocado over and cook for another 5 minutes, or until the bacon is cooked to your liking. Serve on a bed of fresh parsley, if desired, and sprinkle with salt flakes, if desired.

   Best served fresh. Store extras in an airtight container in the fridge for up to 4 days. Reheat in a preheated 320°F air fryer for 4 minutes, or until heated through.

Per serving: Calories **536;** Fat **46g;** Protein **18g;** Total carbs **18g;** Fiber **14g**

Double-Dipped Mini Cinnamon Biscuits

PREP: 15 MINUTES • COOK TIME: 13 MINUTES • TOTAL: 28 MINUTES • SERVES: 8 BISCUITS

Ingredients

2 cups blanched almond flour

½ cup Swerve confectioners'-style sweetener or equivalent amount of liquid or powdered sweetener

1 teaspoon baking powder

½ teaspoon fine sea salt

¼ cup plus 2 tablespoons (¾ stick) very cold unsalted butter

¼ cup unsweetened, unflavored almond milk

1 large egg

1 teaspoon vanilla extract

3 teaspoons ground cinnamon

GLAZE:

½ cup Swerve confectioners'-style sweetener or equivalent amount of powdered sweetener

¼ cup heavy cream or unsweetened, unflavored almond milk

Instructions

1   Preheat the Salter air fryer to 350°F. Line a pie pan that fits into your air fryer with parchment paper. In a medium-sized bowl, mix together the almond flour, sweetener (if powdered; do not add liquid sweetener), baking powder, and salt. Cut the butter into ½-inch squares, then use a hand mixer to work the butter into the dry ingredients. When you are done, the mixture should still have chunks of butter.

In a small bowl, whisk together the almond milk, egg, and vanilla extract (if using liquid sweetener, add it as well) until blended. Using a fork, stir the wet ingredients into the dry ingredients until large clumps form. Add the cinnamon and use your hands to swirl it into the dough. Form the dough into sixteen 1-inch balls and place them on the prepared pan, spacing them about ½ inch apart. (If you're using a smaller air fryer, work in batches if necessary.)

2   Bake in the air fryer until golden, 10 to 13 minutes. Remove from the air fryer and let cool on the pan for at least 5 minutes.

While the biscuits bake, make the glaze: Place the powdered sweetener in a small bowl and slowly stir in the heavy cream with a fork. When the biscuits have cooled somewhat, dip the tops into the glaze, allow it to dry a bit, and then dip again for a thick glaze. Serve warm or at room temperature. Store unglazed biscuits in an airtight container in the refrigerator for up to 3 days or in the freezer for up to a month. Reheat in a preheated 350°F air fryer for 5 minutes, or until warmed through, and dip in the glaze as instructed above.

Per serving: Calories 546; Fat 51g; Protein 14g; Total carbs 13g; Fiber 6g

Foolproof Air Fryer Bacon
PREP: 5 MINUTES • COOK TIME: 10 MINUTES • TOTAL: 15 MINUTES •SERVES: 5

Ingredients
10 slices bacon

Instructions
1 Cut the bacon slices in half, so they will fit in the air fryer.
Place the half-slices in the fryer basket in a single layer. (You may need to cook the bacon in more than one batch.)
2 Set the temperature of your Salter AF to 400°F. Set the timer and fry for 5 minutes. Open the drawer and check the bacon. (The power of the fan may have caused the bacon to fly around during the cooking process. If so, use a fork or tongs to rearrange the slices.)
Reset the timer and fry for 5 minutes more. When the time has elapsed, check the bacon again. If you like your bacon crispier, cook it for another 1 to 2 minutes.

Per Serving: Calories: 87; Fat: 7g; Saturated fat: 2g; Carbohydrate: 0g; Fiber: 0g; Sugar: 0g; Protein: 6g; Iron: 0mg; Sodium: 370mg

Meritage Eggs
PREP: 5 MINUTES • COOK TIME: 8 MINUTES • TOTAL: 13 MINUTES • SERVES: 2

Ingredients
2 teaspoons unsalted butter (or coconut oil for dairy-free), for greasing the ramekins
4 large eggs
2 teaspoons chopped fresh thyme
½ teaspoon fine sea salt

¼ teaspoon ground black pepper
2 tablespoons heavy cream (or unsweetened, unflavored almond milk for dairy-free)
3 tablespoons finely grated Parmesan
Fresh thyme leaves, for garnish (optional)

Instructions
1 Preheat the Salter air fryer to 400°F. Grease two 4-ounce ramekins with the butter. Crack 2 eggs into each ramekin and divide the thyme, salt, and pepper between the ramekins. Pour 1 tablespoon of the heavy cream into each ramekin. Sprinkle each ramekin with 1½ tablespoons of the Parmesan cheese.
2 Place the ramekins in the air fryer and cook for 8 minutes for soft-cooked yolks (longer if you desire a harder yolk). Garnish with a sprinkle of ground black pepper and thyme leaves, if desired. Best served fresh.

Per serving: Calories 331; Fat 29g; Protein 16g; Total carbs 2g; Fiber 0.2g

Easy Air Fryer Buttermilk Biscuits

PREP: 5 MINUTES • COOK TIME: 5 MINUTES • TOTAL: 10 MINUTES • SERVES: 12

Ingredients

2 cups all-purpose flour
1 tablespoon baking powder
¼ teaspoon baking soda
2 teaspoons sugar
1 teaspoon salt

6 tablespoons (¾ stick) cold unsalted butter, cut into 1-tablespoon slices
¾ cup buttermilk
4 tablespoons (½ stick) unsalted butter, melted (optional)

Instructions

1   Spray the Salter air fryer basket with olive oil.
   In a large mixing bowl, combine the flour, baking powder, baking soda, sugar, and salt and mix well.
   Using a fork, cut in the butter until the mixture resembles coarse meal.
   Add the buttermilk and mix until smooth. Sprinkle flour on a clean work surface. Turn the dough out onto the work surface and roll it out until it is about ½ inch thick.
   Using a 2-inch biscuit cutter, cut out the biscuits. Place the uncooked biscuits in the greased Salter air fryer basket in a single layer.
2   Set the temperature of your Salter AF to 360°F. Set the timer and bake for 5 minutes.
   Transfer the cooked biscuits from the air fryer to a platter. Brush the tops with melted butter, if desired. Cut the remaining biscuits (you may have to gather up the scraps of dough and reroll the dough for the last couple of biscuits). Bake the remaining biscuits.
   Plate, serve, and enjoy!

Per Serving (1 biscuit): Calories: 146; Fat: 6g; Saturated fat: 4g; Carbohydrate: 20g; Fiber: 1g; Sugar: 2g; Protein: 3g; Iron: 1mg; Sodium: 280mg

Breakfast Pizza

PREP: 5 MINUTES • COOK TIME: 8 MINUTES • TOTAL: 13 MINUTES • SERVES: 1

Ingredients

2 large eggs
¼ cup unsweetened, unflavored almond milk
¼ teaspoon fine sea salt
⅛ teaspoon ground black pepper
¼ cup diced onions

¼ cup shredded Parmesan cheese
6 pepperoni slices
¼ teaspoon dried oregano leaves
¼ cup pizza sauce, warmed, for serving

Instructions

1   Preheat the Salter air fryer to 350°F. Grease a 6 by 3-inch cake pan.
   In a small bowl, use a fork to whisk together the eggs, almond milk, salt, and pepper. Add the onions and stir to mix. Pour the mixture into the greased pan. Top with the cheese (if using), pepperoni slices (if using), and oregano.
2   Place the pan in the air fryer and cook for 8 minutes, or until the eggs are cooked to your liking.
   Loosen the eggs from the sides of the pan with a spatula and place them on a serving plate. Drizzle the pizza sauce on top. Best served fresh.

Per serving: Calories 357; Fat 25g; Protein 24g; Total carbs 9g; Fiber 2g

Easy Bacon

PREP: 2 MINUTES • COOK TIME: 6 MINUTES • TOTAL: 8 MINUTES • SERVES: 2

Ingredients
4 slices thin-cut bacon or beef bacon

Instructions
1   Spray the Salter air fryer basket with avocado oil. Preheat the Salter air fryer to 360°F.
2   Place the bacon in the Salter air fryer basket in a single layer, spaced about ¼ inch apart Cook for 4 to 6 minutes (thicker bacon will take longer). Check the bacon after 4 minutes to make sure it is not overcooking. Best served fresh. Store extras in an airtight container in the fridge for up to 4 days. Reheat in a preheated 360°F air fryer for 2 minutes, or until heated through.

Per serving: Calories 140; Fat 12g; Protein 8g; Total carbs 0g; Fiber 0g

Blueberry Pancake Poppers

PREP: 5 MINUTES • COOK TIME: 8 MINUTES • TOTAL: 13 MINUTES • SERVES: 8

Ingredients
1 cup all-purpose flour
1 tablespoon sugar
1 teaspoon baking soda
½ teaspoon baking powder
1 cup milk

1 large egg
1 teaspoon vanilla extract
1 teaspoon olive oil
½ cup fresh blueberries

Instructions
1   In a medium mixing bowl, combine the flour, sugar, baking soda, and baking powder and mix well. Mix in the milk, egg, vanilla, and oil. Coat the inside of an air fryer muffin tin with cooking spray. Fill each muffin cup two-thirds full. (You may have to bake the poppers in more than one batch.) Drop a few blueberries into each muffin cup.
Set the muffin tin into the air fryer basket.
2   Set the temperature of your Salter AF to 320°F. Set the timer and bake for 8 minutes. Insert a toothpick into the center of a pancake popper; if it comes out clean, they are done. If batter clings to the toothpick, cook the poppers for 2 minutes more and check again. When the poppers are cooked through, use silicone oven mitts to remove the muffin tin from the air fryer basket. Turn out the poppers onto a wire rack to cool.

Per Serving (1 popper): Calories: 103; Fat: 2g; Saturated fat: 1g; Carbohydrate: 18g; Fiber: 1g; Sugar: 4g; Protein: 4g; Iron: 1mg; Sodium: 181mg

Air Fryer Cinnamon Rolls

PREP: 5 MINUTES • COOK TIME: 12 MINUTES • TOTAL: 17 MINUTES • SERVES: 1

Ingredients

1 can of cinnamon rolls

Instructions

1 Spray the Salter air fryer basket with olive oil.
   Separate the canned cinnamon rolls and place them in the air fryer basket.

2

   Set the temperature of your Salter AF to 340°F. Set the timer and bake for 6 minutes.
   Using tongs, flip the cinnamon rolls. Reset the timer and bake for another 6 minutes.
   When the rolls are done cooking, use tongs to remove them from the air fryer. Transfer them to a platter and spread them with the icing that comes in the package.

Denver Omelet

PREP: 5 MINUTES • COOK TIME: 8 MINUTES • TOTAL: 13 MINUTES • SERVES: 1

Ingredients

2 large eggs
¼ cup unsweetened, unflavored almond milk
¼ teaspoon fine sea salt
⅛ teaspoon ground black pepper
¼ cup diced ham (omit for vegetarian)

¼ cup diced green and red bell peppers
2 tablespoons diced green onions, plus more for garnish
¼ cup shredded cheddar cheese
Quartered cherry tomatoes, for serving

Instructions

1 Preheat the Salter air fryer to 350°F. Grease a 6 by 3-inch cake pan and set aside. In a small bowl, use a fork to whisk together the eggs, almond milk, salt, and pepper. Add the ham, bell peppers, and green onions. Pour the mixture into the greased pan. Add the cheese on top (if using).

2 Place the pan in the basket of the air fryer. Cook for 8 minutes, or until the eggs are cooked to your liking. Loosen the omelet from the sides of the pan with a spatula and place it on a serving plate. Garnish with green onions and serve with cherry tomatoes, if desired. Best served fresh.

Homemade Air Fried Banana Bread

PREP: 5 MINUTES • COOK TIME: 22 MINUTES • TOTAL: 13 MINUTES • SERVES: 3

Ingredients

3 ripe bananas, mashed
1 cup sugar
1 large egg
4 tablespoons (½ stick) unsalted butter, melted

1½ cups all-purpose flour
1 teaspoon baking soda
1 teaspoon salt

Instructions

1 Coat the insides of 3 mini loaf pans with cooking spray. In a large mixing bowl, mix together the bananas and sugar. In a separate large mixing bowl, combine the egg, butter, flour, baking soda, and salt and mix well. Add the banana mixture to the egg and flour mixture. Mix well. Divide the batter evenly among the prepared pans. Set the mini loaf pans into the air fryer basket.

2 Set the temperature of your Salter AF to 310°F. Set the timer and bake for 22 minutes. Insert a toothpick into the center of each loaf; if it comes out clean, they are done. If the batter clings to the toothpick, cook the loaves for 2 minutes more and check again. When the loaves are cooked through, use silicone oven mitts to remove the pans from the air fryer basket. Turn out the loaves onto a wire rack to cool.

Air Fryer Homemade Blueberry Muffins
PREP: 5 MINUTES • COOK TIME: 14 MINUTES • TOTAL: 19 MINUTES • SERVES: 10

Ingredients
⅔ cup all-purpose flour
1 teaspoon baking powder
2 tablespoons sugar
1 egg

2 teaspoons vanilla extract
⅓ cup low-fat milk
3 tablespoons unsalted butter, melted
¾ cup fresh blueberries

Instructions
1 In a medium mixing bowl, combine the flour, baking powder, sugar, egg, vanilla, milk, and melted butter and mix well. Fold in the blueberries. Coat the inside of an air fryer muffin tin with cooking spray. Fill each muffin cup about two-thirds full. Set the muffin tin into the air fryer basket.

2 Set the temperature of your Salter AF to 320°F. Set the timer and bake for 14 minutes.
Insert a toothpick into the center of a muffin; if it comes out clean, they are done. If batter clings to the toothpick, cook the muffins for 2 minutes more and check again. When the muffins are cooked through, use silicone oven mitts to remove the muffin tin from the air fryer basket. Turn out the muffins onto a wire rack to cool slightly before serving.

Per Serving: Calories: 92; Fat: 4g; Saturated fat: 2g; Carbohydrate: 12g; Fiber: 1g; Sugar: 4g; Protein: 2g; Iron: 1mg; Sodium: 35mg

Cheesy Baked Grits
PREP: 10 MINUTES • COOK TIME: 12 MINUTES • TOTAL: 22 MINUTES • SERVES: 6

Ingredients
¾ cup hot water
2 (1-ounce) packages instant grits (⅔ cup)
1 large egg, beaten
1 tablespoon butter, melted

2 cloves garlic, minced
½ to 1 teaspoon red pepper flakes
1 cup shredded cheddar cheese or jalapeño Jack cheese

Instructions
1 In a 6 × 3-inch round heatproof pan, combine the water, grits, egg, butter, garlic, and red pepper flakes. Stir until well combined. Stir in the shredded cheese.

2 Place the pan in the air fryer basket. Set the Salter air fryer to 400°F for 12 minutes, or until the grits have cooked through and a knife inserted near the center comes out clean.
Let stand for 5 minutes before serving.

Easy Mexican Shakshuka
PREP: 5 MINUTES • COOK TIME: 6 MINUTES • TOTAL: 11 MINUTES • SERVES: 1

Ingredients
½ cup salsa
2 large eggs, room temperature
½ teaspoon fine sea salt
¼ teaspoon smoked paprika

⅛ teaspoon ground cumin
FOR GARNISH:
2 tablespoons cilantro leaves

Instructions
1 Preheat the Salter air fryer to 400°F.
Place the salsa in a 6-inch pie pan or a casserole dish that will fit into your air fryer. Crack the eggs into the salsa and sprinkle them with the salt, paprika, and cumin.

2 Place the pan in the air fryer and cook for 6 minutes, or until the egg whites are set and the yolks are cooked to your liking. Remove from the air fryer and garnish with the cilantro before serving.

Per serving: Calories 258; Fat 17g; Protein 14g; Total carbs 11g; Fiber 4g

Appetizers

Bacon-Wrapped Pickle Spears
PREP: 10 MINUTES • COOK TIME: 8 MINUTES • TOTAL: 18 MINUTES •SERVES: 4

Ingredients

8 to 12 slices bacon

¼ cup (2 ounces) cream cheese, softened

¼ cup shredded mozzarella cheese

8 dill pickle spears

½ cup ranch dressing

Instructions

1. Lay the bacon slices on a flat surface. In a medium bowl, combine the cream cheese and mozzarella. Stir until well blended. Spread the cheese mixture over the bacon slices.
   Place a pickle spear on a bacon slice and roll the bacon around the pickle in a spiral, ensuring the pickle is fully covered. (You may need to use more than one slice of bacon per pickle to fully cover the spear.) Tuck in the ends to ensure the bacon stays put. Repeat to wrap all the pickles.
2. Place the wrapped pickles in the Salter air fryer basket in a single layer. Set the Salter air fryer to 400°F for 8 minutes, or until the bacon is cooked through and crisp on the edges.
   Serve the pickle spears with ranch dressing on the side.

Buffalo Cauliflower
PREP: 5 MINUTES • COOK TIME: 11 MINUTES • TOTAL: 16 MINUTES
SERVES: 4

Ingredients

¼ cup hot sauce

¼ cup powdered Parmesan cheese

2 tablespoons unsalted butter, melted

1 small head cauliflower, cut into 1-inch bites

Blue Cheese Dressing, for serving

Blue Cheese Dressing
PREP: 20 MINUTES • COOK TIME: 30 MINUTES • TOTAL: 50 MINUTES
SERVES: 2 CUPS

Ingredients

8 ounces crumbled blue cheese, plus more if desired for a chunky texture

¼ cup beef bone broth

¼ cup full-fat sour cream

¼ cup red wine vinegar or coconut vinegar

1½ tablespoons Swerve confectioners'-style sweetener or equivalent amount of liquid or powdered sweetener

1 tablespoon MCT oil

1clove garlic, peeled

Instructions

1. Place all the ingredients in a food processor and blend until smooth. Transfer to a jar. Stir in extra chunks of blue cheese if desired. Store in the refrigerator for up to 5 days. Preheat the Salter air fryer to 400°F. Spray a baking dish that will fit into your air fryer with avocado oil.
   Place the hot sauce, Parmesan, and butter in a large bowl and stir to combine. Add the cauliflower and toss to coat well.
2. Place the coated cauliflower in the baking dish. Cook in the air fryer for 11 minutes, stirring halfway through. Serve with blue cheese dressing.
   Store leftovers in an airtight container in the fridge for up to 4 days. Reheat in a preheated 400°F oven for 3 minutes, until warmed through and crispy.

Per serving: Calories **185;** Fat **15g;** Protein **9g;** Total carbs **4g;** Fiber **2g**

Ranch Roasted Chickpeas

PREP: 4 MINUTES • COOK TIME: 10 MINUTES • TOTAL: 14 MINUTES • SERVES: 4

Ingredients

1 (15-ounce) can chickpeas, drained and rinsed
1 tablespoon olive oil
3 tablespoons ranch seasoning mix

1 teaspoon salt
2 tablespoons freshly squeezed lemon juice

Instructions

1. Spray the Salter air fryer basket with olive oil.
   Using paper towels, pat the chickpeas dry. In a medium mixing bowl, mix together the chickpeas, oil, seasoning mix, salt, and lemon juice. Put the chickpeas in the Salter air fryer basket and spread them out in a single layer. (You may need to cook the chickpeas in more than one batch.)
2. Set the temperature of your Salter AF to 350°F. Set the timer and roast for 4 minutes. Remove the drawer and shake vigorously to redistribute the chickpeas so they cook evenly. Reset the timer and roast for 6 minutes more. When the time is up, release the Salter air fryer basket from the drawer and pour the chickpeas into a bowl. Season with additional salt, if desired. Enjoy!

Per Serving: Calories: 144; Fat: 5g; Saturated fat: 1g; Carbohydrate: 19g; Fiber: 5g; Sugar: 3g; Protein: 6g; Iron: 2mg; Sodium: 891mg

Caramelized Onion Dip

PREP:5 MINUTES PLUS 2 HOURS TO CHILL•COOK TIME: 30 MINUTES •TOTAL: 2 HOUR 35 MINUTES • SERVES: 8-10

Ingredients

1 tablespoon butter
1 medium yellow onion, halved and thinly sliced
¼ teaspoon kosher salt, plus additional for seasoning
4 ounces cream cheese, softened
½ cup sour cream

¼ teaspoon onion powder
1 tablespoon chopped fresh chives
Black pepper
Thick-cut potato chips or vegetable chips

Instructions

1. Place the butter in a 6 × 3-inch round heatproof pan. Place the pan in the air fryer basket.
2. Set the Salter air fryer to 200°F for 1 minute, or until the butter is melted. Add the onions and salt to the pan. Set the Salter air fryer to 200°F for 15 minutes, or until onions are softened. Set the Salter air fryer to 375°F for 15 minutes, until onions are a deep golden brown, stirring two or three times during the cooking time. Let cool completely. In a medium bowl, stir together the cooked onions, cream cheese, sour cream, onion powder, and chives. Season with salt and pepper. Cover and refrigerate for 2 hours to allow the flavors to blend. Serve the dip with potato chips or vegetable chips.

Homemade Air Fryer Roasted Mixed Nuts

PREP: 5 MINUTES • COOK TIME: 20 MINUTES • TOTAL: 25 MINUTES • SERVES: 6

Ingredients

2 cups mixed nuts (walnuts, pecans, and/or almonds)

2 tablespoons egg white

1 teaspoon ground cinnamon

2 tablespoons sugar

1 teaspoon paprika

Instructions

1. Preheat the Salter air fryer to 300°F and spray the Salter air fryer basket with olive oil. In a small mixing bowl, mix together the nuts, egg white, cinnamon, sugar, and paprika, until the nuts are thoroughly coated.
2. Place the nuts in the greased air fryer basket; set the timer and roast for 10 minutes. After 10 minutes, remove the drawer and shake the basket to redistribute the nuts so they roast evenly. Reset the timer and roast for 10 minutes more. Release the basket from the drawer, pour the nuts into a bowl, and serve.

Per Serving: Calories: 232; Fat: 21g; Saturated fat: 2g; Carbohydrate: 10g; Fiber: 3g; Sugar: 5g; Protein: 6g; Iron: 1mg; Sodium: 6mg

Ranch Kale Chips

PREP: 5 MINUTES • COOK TIME: 10 MINUTES • TOTAL: 15 MINUTES • SERVES: 8 CUPS

Ingredients

½ teaspoon dried chives

½ teaspoon dried dill weed

½ teaspoon dried parsley

¼ teaspoon garlic powder

¼ teaspoon onion powder

⅛ teaspoon fine sea salt

⅛ teaspoon ground black pepper

2 large bunches kale

Instructions

1. Spray the Salter air fryer basket with avocado oil. Preheat the Salter air fryer to 360°F.
   Place the seasonings, salt, and pepper in a small bowl and mix well.
   Wash the kale and pat completely dry. Use a sharp knife to carve out the thick inner stems, then spray the leaves with avocado oil and sprinkle them with the seasoning mix.
2. Place the kale leaves in the air fryer in a single layer and cook for 10 minutes, shaking and rotating the chips halfway through. Transfer the baked chips to a baking sheet to cool completely and crisp up. Repeat with the remaining kale. Sprinkle the cooled chips with salt before serving, if desired.
   Kale chips can be stored in an airtight container at room temperature for up to 1 week, but they are best eaten within 3 days.

Per serving: Calories 11; Fat 0.2g; Protein 1g; Total carbs 2g; Fiber 0.4g

Cheese Drops
PREP: 15 MINUTES • COOK TIME: 10 MINUTES • TOTAL: 25 MINUTES • SERVES: 4

Ingredients

¾ cup all-purpose flour
½ teaspoon kosher salt
¼ teaspoon cayenne pepper
¼ teaspoon smoked paprika
¼ teaspoon black pepper

Dash garlic powder (optional)
¼ cup butter, softened
1 cup shredded sharp cheddar cheese, at room temperature
Olive oil spray

Instructions

1. In a small bowl, combine the flour, salt, cayenne, paprika, pepper, and garlic powder, if using. Using a food processor, cream the butter and cheese until smooth. Gently add the seasoned flour and process until the dough is well combined, smooth, and no longer sticky. (Or make the dough in a stand mixer fitted with the paddle attachment: Cream the butter and cheese on medium speed until smooth, then add the seasoned flour and beat at low speed until smooth.)
   Divide the dough into 32 equal-size pieces. On a lightly floured surface, roll each piece into a small ball.
2. Spray the Salter air fryer basket with oil spray. Arrange 16 cheese drops in the basket. Set the Salter air fryer to 325°F for 10 minutes, or until drops are just starting to brown. Transfer to a wire rack. Repeat with remaining dough, checking for doneness at 8 minutes. Cool the cheese drops completely on the wire rack. Store in an airtight container until ready to serve, or up to 1 or 2 days.

Onion Pakoras
PREP: 5 MINUTES PLUS 30 MINUTES TO STAND • COOK TIME: 10 MINUTES • TOTAL: 45 MINUTES • SERVES: 4

Ingredients

2 medium yellow or white onions, sliced
½ cup chopped fresh cilantro
2 tablespoons vegetable oil
1 tablespoon chickpea flour
1 tablespoon rice flour

1 teaspoon ground turmeric
1 teaspoon cumin seeds
1 teaspoon kosher salt
½ teaspoon cayenne pepper
Vegetable oil spray

Instructions

1. In a large bowl, combine the onions, cilantro, oil, chickpea flour, rice flour, turmeric, cumin seeds, salt, and cayenne. Stir to combine. Cover and let stand for 30 minutes or up to overnight. (This allows the onions to release moisture, creating a batter.) Mix well before using. Spray the Salter air fryer basket generously with vegetable oil spray. Drop half of the batter in 6 heaping tablespoons into the basket.
2. Set the Salter air fryer to 350°F for 8 minutes. Carefully turn the pakoras over and spray with oil spray. Set the Salter air fryer for 2 minutes, or until the batter is cooked through and crisp. Repeat with remaining batter to make 6 more pakoras, checking at 6 minutes for doneness. Serve hot.

Lebanese Muhammara
PREP: 15 MINUTES • COOK TIME: 15 MINUTES • TOTAL: 30 MINUTES • SERVES: 6

Ingredients

2 large red bell peppers
¼ cup plus 2 tablespoons olive oil
1 cup walnut halves
1 tablespoon agave nectar or honey
1 teaspoon fresh lemon juice
1 teaspoon ground cumin

1 teaspoon kosher salt
1 teaspoon red pepper flakes
Raw vegetables (such as cucumber, carrots, zucchini slices, or cauliflower) or toasted pita chips, for serving

Instructions

1. Drizzle the peppers with 2 tablespoons of the olive oil and place in the air fryer basket. Set the Salter air fryer to 400°F for 10 minutes.

2. Add the walnuts to the basket, arranging them around the peppers. Set the Salter air fryer to 400°F for 5 minutes. Remove the peppers, seal in a resealable plastic bag, and let rest for 5 to 10 minutes. Transfer the walnuts to a plate and set aside to cool.

   Place the softened peppers, walnuts, agave, lemon juice, cumin, salt, and ½ teaspoon of the pepper flakes in a food processor and puree until smooth. Transfer the dip to a serving bowl and make an indentation in the middle. Pour the remaining ¼ cup olive oil into the indentation. Garnish the dip with the remaining ½ teaspoon pepper flakes.

   Serve with vegetables or toasted pita chips.

Easy Tomato And Basil Bruschetta
PREP: 5 MINUTES • COOK TIME: 3 MINUTES • TOTAL: 8 MINUTES • SERVES: 6

Ingredients

4 tomatoes, diced
⅓ cup fresh basil, shredded
¼ cup shredded Parmesan cheese
1 tablespoon minced garlic
1 tablespoon balsamic vinegar

1 teaspoon olive oil
1 teaspoon salt
1 teaspoon freshly ground black pepper
1 loaf French bread

Instructions

In a medium mixing bowl, combine the tomatoes and basil.

Mix in the Parmesan cheese, garlic, vinegar, olive oil, salt, and pepper. Let the tomato mixture sit and marinate, while you prepare the bread. Spray the Salter air fryer basket with olive oil. Cut the bread into 1-inch-thick slices. Place the slices in the greased Salter air fryer basket in a single layer. Spray the top of the bread with olive oil. Set the temperature of your Salter AF to 250°F. Set the timer and toast for 3 minutes.

Using tongs, remove the bread slices from the air fryer and place a spoonful of the bruschetta topping on each piece.

Per Serving: Calories: 258; Fat: 3g; Saturated fat: 1g; Carbohydrate: 47g; Fiber: 3g; Sugar: 4g; Protein: 11g; Iron: 3mg; Sodium: 826mg

Crispy Nacho Avocado Fries
PREP: 10 MINUTES • COOK TIME: 15 MINUTES • TOTAL: 25 MINUTES • SERVES: 6

Ingredients

3 firm, barely ripe avocados, halved, peeled, and pitted
2 cups pork dust (or powdered Parmesan cheese for vegetarian)
2 teaspoons fine sea salt
2 teaspoons ground black pepper
2 teaspoons ground cumin
1 teaspoon chili powder

1 teaspoon paprika
½ teaspoon garlic powder
½ teaspoon onion powder
2 large eggs
Salsa, for serving (optional)
Fresh chopped cilantro leaves, for garnish (optional)

Instructions

1. Spray the Salter air fryer basket with avocado oil. Preheat the Salter air fryer to 400°F.
   Slice the avocados into thick-cut french fry shapes.
   In a bowl, mix together the pork dust, salt, pepper, and seasonings.
   In a separate shallow bowl, beat the eggs.
   Dip the avocado fries into the beaten eggs and shake off any excess, then dip them into the pork dust mixture. Use your hands to press the breading into each fry.
   Spray the fries with avocado oil and place them in the Salter air fryer basket in a single layer, leaving space between them. If there are too many fries to fit in a single layer, work in batches.
2. Cook in the air fryer for 13 to 15 minutes, until golden brown, flipping after 5 minutes.
   Serve with salsa, if desired, and garnish with fresh chopped cilantro, if desired. Best served fresh.
   Store leftovers in an airtight container in the fridge for up to 5 days. Reheat in a preheated 400°F air fryer for 3 minutes, or until heated through.

Per serving: Calories 282; Fat 22g; Protein 15g; Total carbs 9g; Fiber 7g

Seasoned Sausage Rolls
PREP: 5 MINUTES • COOK TIME: 5 MINUTES • TOTAL: 10 MINUTES • SERVES: 6

Ingredients

FOR THE SEASONING
2 tablespoons sesame seeds
1½ teaspoons poppy seeds
1½ teaspoons dried minced onion
1 teaspoon salt

1 teaspoon dried minced garlic
FOR THE SAUSAGES
1 (8-ounce) package crescent roll dough
1 (12-ounce) package mini smoked sausages (cocktail franks)

Instructions

1. TO MAKE THE SEASONING: In a small bowl, combine the sesame seeds, poppy seeds, onion, salt, and garlic and set aside.
   TO MAKE THE SAUSAGES. Spray the Salter air fryer basket with olive oil. Remove the crescent dough from the package and lay it out on a cutting board. Separate the dough at the perforations. Using a pizza cutter or sharp knife, cut each triangle of dough into fourths. Drain the sausages and pat them dry with a paper towel. Roll each sausage in a piece of dough. Sprinkle seasoning on top of each roll. Place the seasoned sausage rolls into the greased Salter air fryer basket in a single layer.
2. Set the temperature of your Salter AF to 330°F. Set the timer for 5 minutes. Using tongs, remove the sausages from the air fryer and place them on a platter. Repeat steps 6 through 8 with the second batch.

Per Serving: Calories: 344; Fat: 26g; Saturated fat: 8g; Carbohydrate: 17g; Fiber: 1g; Sugar: 3g; Protein: 10g; Iron: 2mg; Sodium: 1145mg

Homemade Air Fryer Pita Chips
PREP: 5 MINUTES • COOK TIME: 6 MINUTES • TOTAL: 11 MINUTES • SERVES: 4

Ingredients

2 pieces whole wheat pita bread
3 tablespoons olive oil
1 teaspoon freshly squeezed lemon juice

1 teaspoon salt
1 teaspoon dried basil
1 teaspoon garlic powder

Instructions

1. Spray the Salter air fryer basket with olive oil. Using a pair of kitchen shears or a pizza cutter, cut the pita bread into small wedges. Place the wedges in a small mixing bowl and add the olive oil, lemon juice, salt, dried basil, and garlic powder. Mix well, coating each wedge. Place the seasoned pita wedges in the greased Salter air fryer basket in a single layer, being careful not to overcrowd them.
   Set the temperature of your Salter AF to 350°F. Set the timer and bake for 6 minutes. Every 2 minutes or so, remove the drawer and shake the pita chips so they redistribute in the basket for even cooking. Serve with your choice of dip or alone as a tasty snack.

Bacon-Wrapped Pickle Poppers
PREP: 10 MINUTES • COOK TIME: 10 MINUTES • TOTAL: 20 MINUTES • SERVES: 24 POPPERS

Ingredients

12 medium dill pickles
1 (8-ounce) package cream cheese, softened
1 cup shredded sharp cheddar cheese

12 slices bacon or beef bacon, sliced in half lengthwise
Ranch Dressing or Blue Cheese Dressing, for serving (optional)

Instructions

1. Spray the Salter air fryer basket with avocado oil. Preheat the Salter air fryer to 400°F. Slice the dill pickles in half lengthwise and use a spoon to scoop out the centers. Place the cream cheese and cheddar cheese in a small bowl and stir until well combined. Divide the cream cheese mixture among the pickles, spooning equal amounts into the scooped-out centers. Wrap each filled pickle with a slice of bacon and secure the bacon with toothpicks.
2. Place the bacon-wrapped pickles in the Salter air fryer basket with the bacon seam side down and cook for 8 to 10 minutes, until the bacon is crispy, flipping halfway through. Serve warm with ranch or blue cheese dressing, if desired.
   Best served fresh. Store leftovers in an airtight container in the fridge for up to 5 days. Reheat in a preheated 400°F air fryer for 3 minutes, or until heated through.

Per serving: Calories 87; Fat 8g; Protein 4g; Total carbs 1g; Fiber 1g

Doro Wat Wings

PREP: 5 MINUTES • COOK TIME: 32 MINUTES • TOTAL: 37 MINUTES •SERVES: 1 DOZEN WINGS

Ingredients

1 dozen chicken wings or drummies
1 tablespoon coconut oil or bacon fat, melted
2 teaspoons berbere spice
1 teaspoon fine sea salt
FOR SERVING

(OMIT FOR EGG-FREE):
2 hard-boiled eggs
½ teaspoon fine sea salt
¼ teaspoon berbere spice
¼ teaspoon dried chives

Instructions

1. Spray the Salter air fryer basket with avocado oil. Preheat the Salter air fryer to 380°F.
   Place the chicken wings in a large bowl. Pour the oil over them and turn to coat completely. Sprinkle the berbere and salt on all sides of the chicken.
2. Place the chicken wings in the air fryer and cook for 25 minutes, flipping after 15 minutes.
   After 25 minutes, increase the temperature to 400°F and cook for 6 to 7 minutes more, until the skin is browned and crisp.
   While the chicken cooks, prepare the hard-boiled eggs (if using): Peel the eggs, slice them in half, and season them with the salt, berbere, and dried chives. Serve the chicken and eggs together.

Per serving: Calories 317; Fat 24g; Protein 24g; Total carbs 0.1g; Fiber 0g

Bourbon Chicken Wings

PREP: 10 MINUTES • COOK TIME: 32 MINUTES • TOTAL: 42 MINUTES • SERVES: 8

Ingredients

2 pounds chicken wings or drummies
½ teaspoon fine sea salt
SAUCE:
½ cup chicken broth
⅓ cup Swerve confectioners'-style sweetener or equivalent amount of liquid or powdered sweetener
¼ cup tomato sauce
¼ cup wheat-free tamari

1 tablespoon apple cider vinegar
¾ teaspoon red pepper flakes
¼ teaspoon grated fresh ginger
1 clove garlic, smashed to a paste
FOR GARNISH (OPTIONAL):
Chopped green onions
Sesame seeds

Instructions

1. Spray the Salter air fryer basket with avocado oil. Preheat the Salter air fryer to 380°F.
   Season the chicken wings on all sides with the salt and place them in the air fryer.
2. Cook for 25 minutes, flipping after 15 minutes. After 25 minutes, increase the temperature to 400°F and cook for 6 to 7 minutes more, until the skin is browned and crisp.

Vegetables Recipes

Air Fryer Asparagus
PREP: 5 MINUTES • COOK TIME: 8 MINUTES • TOTAL: 13 MINUTES • SERVES: 2

Ingredients

Nutritional yeast

Olive oil non-stick spray

One bunch of asparagus

Instructions

Wash asparagus and then trim off thick, woody ends. Spray asparagus with olive oil spray and sprinkle with yeast. In your Air fryer, lay asparagus in a singular layer. Set the temperature of your Salter AF to 360°F, and set time to 8 minutes.

Simple Roasted Garlic Asparagus
PREP: 5 MINUTES • COOK TIME: 10 MINUTES • TOTAL: 15 MINUTES • SERVES: 4

Ingredients

1 pound asparagus

2 tablespoons olive oil

1 tablespoon balsamic vinegar

2 teaspoons minced garlic

Salt

Freshly ground black pepper

Instructions

1. Cut or snap off the white end of the asparagus.
   In a large bowl, combine the asparagus, olive oil, vinegar, garlic, salt, and pepper.
   Using your hands, gently mix all the ingredients together, making sure that the asparagus is thoroughly coated.
   Lay out the asparagus in the Salter air fryer basket or on an air fryer–size baking sheet set in the basket.
2. Set the temperature of your Salter AF to 400°F. Set the timer and roast for 5 minutes.
   Using tongs, flip the asparagus. Reset the timer and roast for 5 minutes more.

Per Serving: Calories: 86; Fat: 7g; Saturated fat: 1g; Carbohydrate: 5g; Fiber: 2g; Sugar: 2g; Protein: 3g; Iron: 2mg; Sodium: 41mg

Ranch Kale Chips
PREP: 5 MINUTES • COOK TIME: 10 MINUTES • TOTAL: 15 MINUTES • SERVES: 8 CUPS

Ingredients

½ teaspoon dried chives

½ teaspoon dried dill weed

½ teaspoon dried parsley

¼ teaspoon garlic powder

¼ teaspoon onion powder

⅛ teaspoon fine sea salt

⅛ teaspoon ground black pepper

2 large bunches kale

Instructions

1. Spray the Salter air fryer basket with avocado oil. Preheat the Salter air fryer to 360°F.
   Place the seasonings, salt, and pepper in a small bowl and mix well. Wash the kale and pat completely dry. Use a sharp knife to carve out the thick inner stems, then spray the leaves with avocado oil and sprinkle them with the seasoning mix.
2. Place the kale leaves in the air fryer in a single layer and cook for 10 minutes, shaking and rotating the chips halfway through. Transfer the baked chips to a baking sheet to cool completely and crisp up. Repeat with the remaining kale. Sprinkle the cooled chips with salt before serving, if desired.
   Kale chips can be stored in an airtight container at room temperature for up to 1 week, but they are best eaten within 3 days.

Per serving: Calories 11; Fat 0.2g; Protein 1g; Total carbs 2g; Fiber 0.4g

Almond Flour Battered And Crisped Onion Rings
PREP: 5 MINUTES • COOK TIME: 15 MINUTES • TOTAL: 20 MINUTES • SERVES: 3

Ingredients

½ cup almond flour
¾ cup coconut milk
1 big white onion, sliced into rings
1 egg, beaten

1 tablespoon baking powder
1 tablespoon smoked paprika
Salt and pepper to taste

Instructions

1. Preheat the Salter air fryer for 5 minutes. In a mixing bowl, mix the almond flour, baking powder, smoked paprika, salt and pepper. In another bowl, combine the eggs and coconut milk. Soak the onion slices into the egg mixture.
    Dredge the onion slices in the almond flour mixture.
2. Place in the air fryer basket. Close and cook for 15 minutes at 325 °F.
    Halfway through the cooking time, shake the fryer basket for even cooking.

Per Serving: Calories: 217; Fat: 17.9g; Protein: 5.3g

Crispy Nacho Avocado Fries
PREP: 10 MINUTES • COOK TIME: 15 MINUTES • TOTAL: 25 MINUTES • SERVES: 6

Ingredients

3 firm, barely ripe avocados, halved, peeled, and
 pitted
2 cups pork dust
2 teaspoons fine sea salt
2 teaspoons ground black pepper
2 teaspoons ground cumin
1 teaspoon chili powder

1 teaspoon paprika
½ teaspoon garlic powder
½ teaspoon onion powder
2 large eggs
Salsa, for serving (optional)
Fresh chopped cilantro leaves, for garnish (optional)

Instructions

1. Spray the Salter air fryer basket with avocado oil. Preheat the Salter air fryer to 400°F.
    Slice the avocados into thick-cut french fry shapes. In a bowl, mix together the pork dust, salt, pepper, and seasonings. In a separate shallow bowl, beat the eggs.
    Dip the avocado fries into the beaten eggs and shake off any excess, then dip them into the pork dust mixture. Use your hands to press the breading into each fry.
    Spray the fries with avocado oil and place them in the Salter air fryer basket in a single layer, leaving space between them. If there are too many fries to fit in a single layer, work in batches.
2.
    Cook in the air fryer for 13 to 15 minutes, until golden brown, flipping after 5 minutes.
    Serve with salsa, if desired, and garnish with fresh chopped cilantro, if desired. Best served fresh. Store leftovers in an airtight container in the fridge for up to 5 days. Reheat in a preheated 400°F air fryer for 3 minutes, or until heated through.

Per serving: Calories 282; Fat 22g; Protein 15g; Total carbs 9g; Fiber 7g

Chermoula-Roasted Beets

PREP: 15 MINUTES • COOK TIME: 25 MINUTES • TOTAL: 40 MINUTES • SERVES: 4

Ingredients

For the Chermoula
1 cup packed fresh cilantro leaves
½ cup packed fresh parsley leaves
6 cloves garlic, peeled
2 teaspoons smoked paprika
2 teaspoons ground cumin
1 teaspoon ground coriander
½ to 1 teaspoon cayenne pepper

Pinch crushed saffron (optional)
½ cup extra-virgin olive oil
Kosher salt
For the Beets
3 medium beets, trimmed, peeled, and cut into 1-inch chunks
2 tablespoons chopped fresh cilantro
2 tablespoons chopped fresh parsley

Instructions

1. *For the chermoula*: In a food processor, combine the cilantro, parsley, garlic, paprika, cumin, coriander, and cayenne. Pulse until coarsely chopped. Add the saffron, if using, and process until combined. With the food processor running, slowly add the olive oil in a steady stream; process until the sauce is uniform. Season to taste with salt.
   For the beets: In a large bowl, drizzle the beets with ½ cup of the chermoula, or enough to coat.
2. Arrange the beets in the air fryer basket. Set the Salter air fryer to 375°F for 25 to minutes, or until the beets are tender. Transfer the beets to a serving platter. Sprinkle with chopped cilantro and parsley and serve.

Jalapeño Poppers

PREP: 10 MINUTES • COOK TIME: 10 MINUTES • TOTAL: 20 MINUTES • SERVES: 4

Ingredients

12-18 whole fresh jalapeño
1 cup nonfat refried beans
1 cup shredded Monterey Jack or extra-sharp cheddar cheese
1 scallion, sliced

1 teaspoon salt, divided
1/4 cup all-purpose flour
2 large eggs
1/2 cup fine cornmeal
Olive oil or canola oil cooking spray

Instructions

1 Start by slicing each jalapeño lengthwise on one side. Place the jalapeños side by side in a microwave safe bowl and microwave them until they are slightly soft; usually around 5 minutes. While your jalapeños cook; mix refried beans, scallions, 1/2 teaspoon salt, and cheese in a bowl. Once your jalapeños are softened you can scoop out the seeds and add one tablespoon of your refried bean mixture. Press the jalapeño closed around the filling. Beat your eggs in a small bowl and place your flour in a separate bowl. In a third bowl mix your cornmeal and the remaining salt in a third bowl. Roll each pepper in the flour, then dip it in the egg, and finally roll it in the cornmeal making sure to coat the entire pepper. Place the peppers on a flat surface and coat them with a cooking spray; olive oil cooking spray is suggested.
2 Cook in your Air fryer at 400 degrees for 5 minutes, turn each pepper, and then cook for another 5 minutes; serve hot.

Fried Plantains

PREP: 10 MINUTES • COOK TIME: 8 MINUTES • TOTAL: 18 MINUTES • SERVES: 2

Ingredients

2 ripe plantains, peeled and cut at a diagonal into ½-inch-thick pieces

3 tablespoons ghee, melted
¼ teaspoon kosher salt

Instructions

1. In a medium bowl, toss the plantains with the ghee and salt.
2. Arrange the plantain pieces in the air fryer basket. Set the Salter air fryer to 400°F for 8 minutes. The plantains are done when they are soft and tender on the inside, and have plenty of crisp, sweet, brown spots on the outside.

Bacon-Wrapped Asparagus

PREP: 5 MINUTES • COOK TIME: 10 MINUTES • TOTAL: 15 MINUTES • SERVES: 4

Ingredients

1 pound asparagus, trimmed (about 24 spears)
4 slices bacon or beef bacon
½ cup Ranch Dressin for serving

3 tablespoons chopped fresh chives, for garnish

Instructions

1. Spray the Salter air fryer basket with avocado oil. Preheat the Salter air fryer to 400°F.
   Slice the bacon down the middle, making long, thin strips. Wrap 1 slice of bacon around 3 asparagus spears and secure each end with a toothpick. Repeat with the remaining bacon and asparagus.
2. Place the asparagus bundles in the air fryer in a single layer. (If you're using a smaller air fryer, cook in batches if necessary.) Cook for 8 minutes for thin stalks, 10 minutes for medium to thick stalks, or until the asparagus is slightly charred on the ends and the bacon is crispy.
   Serve with ranch dressing and garnish with chives. Best served fresh.

Per serving: Calories 241; Fat 22g; Protein 7g; Total carbs 6g; Fiber 3g

Air Fried Roasted Corn on The Cob

PREP: 5 MINUTES • COOK TIME: 10 MINUTES • TOTAL: 15 MINUTES • SERVES: 4

Ingredients

1 tablespoon vegetable oil
4 ears of corn, husks and silk removed
Unsalted butter, for topping

Salt, for topping
Freshly ground black pepper, for topping

Instructions

1. Rub the vegetable oil onto the corn, coating it thoroughly.
2. Set the temperature of your Salter AF to 400°F. Set the timer and grill for 5 minutes.
   Using tongs, flip or rotate the corn.
   Reset the timer and grill for 5 minutes more.
   Serve with a pat of butter and a generous sprinkle of salt and pepper.

Per Serving: Calories: 265; Fat: 17g; Saturated fat: 8g; Carbohydrate: 29g; Fiber: 4g; Sugar: 5g; Protein: 5g; Iron: 4mg; Sodium: 252mg

Parmesan Breaded Zucchini Chips

PREP: 15 MINUTES • COOK TIME: 20 MINUTES • TOTAL: 35 MINUTES • SERVES: 5

Ingredients

For the zucchini chips:
2 medium zucchini
2 eggs
⅓ cup bread crumbs
⅓ cup grated Parmesan cheese
Salt
Pepper
Cooking oil

For the lemon aioli:
½ cup mayonnaise
½ tablespoon olive oil
Juice of ½ lemon
1 teaspoon minced garlic
Salt
Pepper

Instructions

1. To make the zucchini chips: Slice the zucchini into thin chips (about ⅛ inch thick) using a knife or mandoline. In a small bowl, beat the eggs. In another small bowl, combine the bread crumbs, Parmesan cheese, and salt and pepper to taste. Spray the Salter air fryer basket with cooking oil. Dip the zucchini slices one at a time in the eggs and then the bread crumb mixture. You can also sprinkle the bread crumbs onto the zucchini slices with a spoon. Place the zucchini chips in the Air fryer basket, but do not stack.

2. Cook in batches. Spray the chips with cooking oil from a distance (otherwise, the breading may fly off). Cook for 10 minutes. Remove the cooked zucchini chips from the air fryer, then repeat step 5 with the remaining zucchini.

To make the lemon aioli: While the zucchini is cooking, combine the mayonnaise, olive oil, lemon juice, and garlic in a small bowl, adding salt and pepper to taste. Mix well until fully combined. Cool the zucchini and serve alongside the aioli.

Per Serving: Calories: 192; Fat: 13g; Protein: 6g; Fiber: 4g

Green Beans & Bacon

PREP: 10 MINUTES • COOK TIME: 20 MINUTES • TOTAL: 35 MINUTES • SERVES: 4

Ingredients

3 cups frozen cut green beans
1 medium onion, chopped
3 slices bacon, chopped

¼ cup water
Kosher salt and black pepper

Instructions

1. In a 6 × 3-inch round heatproof pan, combine the frozen green beans, onion, bacon, and water. Toss to combine. Place the pan in the air fryer basket.

2. Set the Salter air fryer to 375°F for 15 minutes.
    Raise the air fryer temperature to 400°F for 5 minutes. Season the beans with salt and pepper to taste and toss well.
    Remove the pan from the Salter air fryer basket and cover with foil. Let the beans rest for 5 minutes before serving.

Bell Pepper-Corn Wrapped in Tortilla
PREP: 5 MINUTES • COOK TIME: 15 MINUTES • TOTAL: 20 MINUTES • SERVES: 4

Ingredients

1 small red bell pepper, chopped
1 small yellow onion, diced
1 tablespoon water
2 cobs grilled corn kernels

4 large tortillas
4 pieces commercial vegan nuggets, chopped
mixed greens for garnish

Instructions

1. Preheat the Salter air fryer to 400°F. In a skillet heated over medium heat, water sauté the vegan nuggets together with the onions, bell peppers, and corn kernels. Set aside.

   Place filling inside the corn tortillas.

2. Fold the tortillas and place inside the air fryer and cook for 15 minutes until the tortilla wraps are crispy. Serve with mix greens on top.

Bloomin' Onion
PREP: 10 MINUTES • COOK TIME: 35 MINUTES • TOTAL: 45 MINUTES • SERVES: 8

Ingredients

1 extra-large onion
2 large eggs
1 tablespoon water
½ cup powdered Parmesan cheese
2 teaspoons paprika
1 teaspoon garlic powder
¼ teaspoon cayenne pepper
¼ teaspoon fine sea salt

¼ teaspoon ground black pepper
FOR GARNISH (OPTIONAL):
Fresh parsley leaves
Powdered Parmesan cheese
FOR SERVING (OPTIONAL):
Prepared yellow mustard
Ranch Dressing
Reduced-sugar or sugar-free ketchup

Instructions

1. Spray the Salter air fryer basket with avocado oil. Preheat the Salter air fryer to 350°F.

   Using a sharp knife, cut the top ½ inch off the onion and peel off the outer layer. Cut the onion into 8 equal sections, stopping 1 inch from the bottom—you want the onion to stay together at the base. Gently spread the sections, or "petals," apart.

   Crack the eggs into a large bowl, add the water, and whisk well. Place the onion in the dish and coat it well in the egg. Use a spoon to coat the inside of the onion and all of the petals.

   In a small bowl, combine the Parmesan, seasonings, salt, and pepper.

   Place the onion in a 6-inch pie pan or casserole dish. Sprinkle the seasoning mixture all over the onion and use your fingers to press it into the petals. Spray the onion with avocado oil.

   Loosely cover the onion with parchment paper and then foil.

2. Place the dish in the air fryer. Cook for 30 minutes, then remove it from the air fryer and increase the air fryer temperature to 400°F.

   Remove the foil and parchment and spray the onion with avocado oil again. Protecting your hands with oven-safe gloves or a tea towel, transfer the onion to the air fryer basket. Cook for an additional 3 to 5 minutes, until light brown and crispy.

   Garnish with fresh parsley and powdered Parmesan, if desired. Serve with mustard, ranch dressing, and ketchup, if desired.

   Store leftovers in an airtight container in the fridge for up to 4 days. Reheat in a preheated 400°F air fryer for 3 to 5 minutes, until warm and crispy.

Per serving: Calories 51; Fat 3g; Protein 4g; Total carbs 3g; Fiber 0.4g

Mexican Corn In A Cup
PREP: 5 MINUTES • COOK TIME: 10 MINUTES • TOTAL: 15 MINUTES • SERVES: 4

Ingredients

4 cups (32-ounce bag) frozen corn kernels (do not thaw)
Vegetable oil spray
2 tablespoons butter
¼ cup sour cream
¼ cup mayonnaise

¼ cup grated Parmesan cheese (or feta, cotija, or queso fresco)
2 tablespoons fresh lemon or lime juice
1 teaspoon chili powder
Chopped fresh green onion (optional)
Chopped fresh cilantro (optional)

Instructions

1. Place the corn in the bottom of the Salter air fryer basket and spray with vegetable oil spray.
2. Set the Salter air fryer to 350°F for 10 minutes.
   Transfer the corn to a serving bowl. Add the butter and stir until melted. Add the sour cream, mayonnaise, cheese, lemon juice, and chili powder; stir until well combined. Serve immediately with green onion and cilantro (if using).

Air Fried Honey Roasted Carrots
PREP: 5 MINUTES • COOK TIME: 12 MINUTES • TOTAL: 17 MINUTES • SERVES: 4

Ingredients

3 cups baby carrots
1 tablespoon extra-virgin olive oil
1 tablespoon honey

Salt
Freshly ground black pepper
Fresh dill (optional)

Instructions

1. In a large bowl, combine the carrots, olive oil, honey, salt, and pepper. Make sure that the carrots are thoroughly coated with oil. Place the carrots in the air fryer basket.
2. Set the temperature of your Salter AF to 390°F. Set the timer and roast for 12 minutes, or until fork-tender. Remove the air fryer drawer and release the air fryer basket. Pour the carrots into a bowl, sprinkle with dill, if desired, and serve.

Crispy Sesame-Ginger Broccoli
PREP: 10 MINUTES • COOK TIME: 15 MINUTES • TOTAL: 25 MINUTES • SERVES: 4

Ingredients

3 tablespoons toasted sesame oil
2 teaspoons sesame seeds
1 tablespoon chili-garlic sauce
2 teaspoons minced fresh ginger

½ teaspoon kosher salt
½ teaspoon black pepper
1 (16-ounce) package frozen broccoli florets (do not thaw)

Instructions

1. In a large bowl, combine the sesame oil, sesame seeds, chili-garlic sauce, ginger, salt, and pepper. Stir until well combined. Add the broccoli and toss until well coated.
2. Arrange the broccoli in the air fryer basket. Set the Salter air fryer to 325°F for 15 minutes, or until the broccoli is crisp, tender, and the edges are lightly browned, gently tossing halfway through the cooking time.

Poultry Recipes

Korean Chicken Wings
PREP: 5 MINUTES • COOK TIME: 10 MINUTES • TOTAL: 15 MINUTES • SERVES: 8

Ingredients

Wings:
1 tsp. pepper
1 tsp. salt
2 pounds chicken wings
Sauce:
2 packets Splenda
1 tbsp. minced garlic
1 tbsp. minced ginger

1 tbsp. sesame oil
1 tsp. agave nectar
1 tbsp. mayo
2 tbsp. gochujang
Finishing:
¼ C. chopped green onions
2 tsp. sesame seeds

Instructions:

1 Ensure air fryer is preheated to 400 degrees.
Line a small pan with foil and place a rack onto the pan, then place into air fryer.
Season wings with pepper and salt and place onto the rack.

2 Set temperature to 160°F, and set time to 20 minutes and air fry 20 minutes, turning at 10 minutes. As chicken air fries, mix together all the sauce components.
Once a thermometer says that the chicken has reached 160 degrees, take out wings and place into a bowl. Pour half of the sauce mixture over wings, tossing well to coat. Put coated wings back into air fryer for 5 minutes or till they reach 165 degrees. Remove and sprinkle with green onions and sesame seeds. Dip into extra sauce.

Per Serving: Calories: 356; Fat: 26g; Protein:23g; Sugar:2g

Buffalo Chicken Wings
PREP: 10 MINUTES • COOK TIME: 24 MINUTES • TOTAL: 34 MINUTES • SERVES: 4

Ingredients

8 tablespoons (1 stick) unsalted butter, melted
½ cup hot sauce
2 tablespoons white vinegar
2 teaspoons Worcestershire sauce

1 teaspoon garlic powder
½ cup all-purpose flour
16 frozen chicken wings

Instructions:

1 Preheat the Salter air fryer to 370°F.
In a small saucepan over low heat, combine the butter, hot sauce, vinegar, Worcestershire sauce, and garlic. Mix well and bring to a simmer.
Pour the flour into a medium mixing bowl. Dredge the chicken wings in the flour.
Place the flour-coated wings into the air fryer basket.

2 Set the timer and fry for 12 minutes. Using tongs, flip the wings.
Reset the timer and fry for 12 minutes more.
Release the Salter air fryer basket from the drawer. Turn out the chicken wings into a large mixing bowl, then pour the sauce over them.
Serve and enjoy.

Per Serving: Calories: 705; Fat: 55g; Saturated fat: 23g; Carbohydrate: 14g; Fiber: 1g; Sugar: 1g; Protein: 38g; Iron: 3mg; Sodium: 1096mg

Almond Flour Coco-Milk Battered Chicken

PREP: 5 MINUTES • COOK TIME: 30 MINUTES • TOTAL: 35 MINUTES • SERVES: 4

Ingredients

¼ cup coconut milk
½ cup almond flour
1 ½ tablespoons old bay Cajun seasoning

1 egg, beaten
4 small chicken thighs
Salt and pepper to taste

Instructions:

1 Preheat the Salter air fryer for 5 minutes. Mix the egg and coconut milk in a bowl.
   Soak the chicken thighs in the beaten egg mixture. In a mixing bowl, combine the almond flour, Cajun seasoning, salt and pepper. Dredge the chicken thighs in the almond flour mixture. Place in the air fryer basket.

2 Cook for 30 minutes at 350°F.

Harissa-Rubbed Cornish Game Hens

PREP: 10 MINUTES PLUS 30 MINUTES TO MARINATE • COOK TIME: 20 MINUTES • TOTAL: 60 MINUTES • SERVES: 4

Ingredients

For the Harissa
½ cup olive oil
6 cloves garlic, minced
2 tablespoons smoked paprika
1 tablespoon ground coriander
1 tablespoon ground cumin
1 teaspoon ground caraway

1 teaspoon kosher salt
½ to 1 teaspoon cayenne pepper
For the Hens
½ cup yogurt
Cornish game hens, any giblets removed, split in half lengthwise

Instructions:

1 For the harissa: In a medium microwave-safe bowl, combine the oil, garlic, paprika, coriander, cumin, caraway, salt, and cayenne. Microwave on high for 1 minute, stirring halfway through the cooking time. (You can also heat this on the stovetop until the oil is hot and bubbling. Or, if you must use your air fryer for everything, cook it in the air fryer at 350°F for 5 to 6 minutes, or until the paste is heated through.)
   For the hens: In a small bowl, combine 1 to 2 tablespoons harissa and the yogurt. Whisk until well combined. Place the hen halves in a resealable plastic bag and pour the marinade over. Seal the bag and massage until all of the pieces are thoroughly coated. Marinate at room temperature for 30 minutes or in the refrigerator for up to 24 hours.

2 Arrange the hen halves in a single layer in the air fryer basket. (If you have a smaller air fryer, you may have to cook this in two batches.) Set the Salter air fryer to 400°F for 20 minutes. Use a meat thermometer to ensure the game hens have reached an internal temperature.

Per Serving: Calories: 590; Fat: 38g; Protein:32.5g; Carbs:3.2g

Parmesan Chicken Tenders

PREP: 5 MINUTES • COOK TIME: 8 MINUTES • TOTAL: 13 MINUTES • SERVES: 4

Ingredients

1 pound chicken tenderloins

3 large egg whites

½ cup Italian-style bread crumbs

¼ cup grated Parmesan cheese

Instructions:

1. Spray the Salter air fryer basket with olive oil. Trim off any white fat from the chicken tenders. In a small bowl, beat the egg whites until frothy. In a separate small mixing bowl, combine the bread crumbs and Parmesan cheese. Mix well. Dip the chicken tenders into the egg mixture, then into the Parmesan and bread crumbs. Shake off any excess breading. Place the chicken tenders in the greased Salter air fryer basket in a single layer. Generously spray the chicken with olive oil to avoid powdery, uncooked breading.

2. Set the temperature of your Salter AF to 370°F. Set the timer and bake for 4 minutes. Using tongs, flip the chicken tenders and bake for 4 minutes more. Check that the chicken has reached an internal temperature of 165°F. Add cooking time if needed. Once the chicken is fully cooked, plate, serve, and enjoy.

Per Serving: Calories: 210; Fat: 4g; Saturated fat: 1g; Carbohydrate: 10g; Fiber: 1g; Sugar: 1g; Protein: 33g; Iron: 1mg; Sodium: 390mg

Air Fryer Grilled Chicken Fajitas

PREP: 10 MINUTES • COOK TIME: 14 MINUTES • TOTAL: 24 MINUTES • SERVES: 4

Ingredients

1 pound chicken tenders

1 onion, sliced

1 yellow bell pepper, diced

1 red bell pepper, diced

1 orange bell pepper, diced

2 tablespoons olive oil

1 tablespoon fajita seasoning mix

Instructions:

1. Slice the chicken into thin strips. In a large mixing bowl, combine the chicken, onion, and peppers. Add the olive oil and fajita seasoning and mix well, so that the chicken and vegetables are thoroughly covered with oil. Place the chicken and vegetable mixture into the Salter air fryer basket in a single layer.

2. Set the temperature of your Salter AF to 350°F. Set the timer and grill for 7 minutes.
   Shake the basket and use tongs to flip the chicken. Reset the timer and grill for 7 minutes more, or until the chicken is cooked through and the juices run clear. Once the chicken is fully cooked, transfer it to a platter and serve.

One-Dish Chicken & Rice

PREP: 10 MINUTES • COOK TIME: 40 MINUTES • TOTAL: 50 MINUTES • SERVES: 4

Ingredients

1 cup long-grain white rice

1 cup cut frozen green beans

1 tablespoon minced fresh ginger

3 cloves garlic, minced

1 tablespoon toasted sesame oil

1 teaspoon kosher salt

1 teaspoon black pepper

1pound chicken wings

Instructions:

1. In a 6 × 3-inch round heatproof pan, combine the rice, green beans, ginger, garlic, sesame oil, salt, and pepper. Stir to combine. Place the chicken wings on top of the rice mixture. Cover the pan with foil. Make a long slash in the foil to allow the pan to vent steam.

2. Place the pan in the air fryer basket. Set the Salter air fryer to 375°F for 30 minutes. Remove the foil. Set the Salter air fryer to 400°F for 10 minutes, or until the wings have browned and rendered fat into the rice and vegetables, turning the wings halfway through the cooking time.

Lebanese Turkey Burgers with Feta & Tzatziki
PREP: 25 MINUTES • COOK TIME: 12 MINUTES • TOTAL: 37 MINUTES • SERVES: 4

Ingredients

For the Tzatziki

1 large cucumber, peeled and grated
2 to 3 cloves garlic, minced
1 cup plain Greek yogurt
1 tablespoon tahini (sesame paste)
1 tablespoon fresh lemon juice
½ teaspoon kosher salt

For the Burgers

1 pound ground turkey, chicken, or lamb
1 small yellow onion, finely diced
1 clove garlic, minced

2 tablespoons chopped fresh parsley
2 teaspoons Lebanese Seven-Spice Mix
½ teaspoon kosher salt
Vegetable oil spray

For Serving

4 lettuce leaves or 2 whole-wheat pita breads, halved
8 slices ripe tomato
1 cup baby spinach
⅓ cup crumbled feta cheese

Instructions:

1 *For the tzatziki*: In a medium bowl, stir together all the ingredients until well combined. Cover and chill until ready to serve.
   For the burgers: In a large bowl, combine the ground turkey, onion, garlic, parsley, spice mix, and salt. Mix gently until well combined. Divide the turkey into four portions and form into round patties.
2 Spray the Salter air fryer basket with vegetable oil spray. Place the patties in a single layer in the air fryer basket. Set the Salter air fryer to 400°F for 12 minutes. Place one burger in each lettuce leaf or pita half. Tuck in 2 tomato slices, spinach, cheese, and some tzatziki.

Sweet And Sour Chicken
PREP: 5 MINUTES • COOK TIME: 20 MINUTES • TOTAL: 25 MINUTES • SERVES: 6

Ingredients

3 Chicken Breasts, cubed
1/2 Cup Flour
1/2 Cup Cornstarch
2 Red Peppers, sliced
1 Onion, chopped
2 Carrots, julienned

3/4 Cup Sugar
2 Tbsps Cornstarch
1/3 Cup Vinegar
2/3 Cup Water
1/4 cup Soy sauce
1 Tbsp Ketchup

Instructions:

1. Preheat the Salter air fryer to 375 degrees.
   Combine the flour, cornstarch and chicken in an air tight container and shake to combine. Remove chicken from the container and shake off any excess flour.
2. Add chicken to the Air Fryer tray and cook for 20 minutes.
   In a saucepan, whisk together sugar, water, vinegar, soy sauce and ketchup. Bring to a boil over medium heat, reduce the heat then simmer for 2 minutes. After cooking the chicken for 20 minutes, add the vegetables and sauce mixture to the Air fryer and cook for another 5 minutes. Serve over hot rice

Easy Lemon Chicken Thighs

PREP: 5 MINUTES • COOK TIME: 10 MINUTES • TOTAL: 15 MINUTES • SERVES: 4

Ingredients

1 teaspoon salt
1 teaspoon freshly ground black pepper
2 tablespoons olive oil

2 tablespoons Italian seasoning
2 tablespoons freshly squeezed lemon juice
1 lemon, sliced

Instructions:

1   Place the chicken thighs in a medium mixing bowl and season them with the salt and pepper. Add the olive oil, Italian seasoning, and lemon juice and toss until the chicken thighs are thoroughly coated with oil. Add the sliced lemons. Place the chicken thighs into the Salter air fryer basket in a single layer.

2   Set the temperature of your Salter AF to 350°F. Set the timer and cook for 10 minutes. Using tongs, flip the chicken. Reset the timer and cook for 10 minutes more. Check that the chicken has reached an internal temperature of 165°F. Add cooking time if needed. Once the chicken is fully cooked, plate, serve, and enjoy.

Per Serving: Calories: 325; Fat: 26g; Saturated fat: 6g; Carbohydrate: 1g; Fiber: 0g; Sugar: 1g; Protein: 20g; Iron: 1mg; Sodium: 670mg

Air Fryer Southern Fried Chicken

PREP:15 MINUTES PLUS 1HOUR TO MARINATE•COOK TIME: 26 MINUTES •TOTAL:1 HOUR 36 MINUTES•SERVES: 4

Ingredients

½ cup buttermilk
2 teaspoons salt, plus 1 tablespoon
1 teaspoon freshly ground black pepper
1 pound chicken thighs and drumsticks

1 cup all-purpose flour
2 teaspoons onion powder
2 teaspoons garlic powder
½ teaspoon sweet paprika

Instructions:

1   In a large mixing bowl, whisk together the buttermilk, 2 teaspoons of salt, and pepper. Add the chicken pieces to the bowl, and let the chicken marinate for at least an hour, covered, in the refrigerator. About 5 minutes before the chicken is done marinating, prepare the dredging mixture. In a large mixing bowl, combine the flour, 1 tablespoon of salt, onion powder, garlic powder, and paprika. Spray the Salter air fryer basket with olive oil. Remove the chicken from the buttermilk mixture and dredge it in the flour mixture. Shake off any excess flour. Place the chicken pieces into the greased Salter air fryer basket in a single layer, leaving space between each piece. Spray the chicken generously with olive oil.

2   Set the temperature of your Salter AF to 390°F. Set the timer and cook for 13 minutes. Using tongs, flip the chicken. Spray generously with olive oil. Reset the timer and fry for 13 minutes more. Check that the chicken has reached an internal temperature of 165°F. Add cooking time if needed. Once the chicken is fully cooked, plate, serve, and enjoy!

Per Serving: Calories: 377; Fat: 18g; Saturated fat: 5g; Carbohydrate: 28g; Fiber: 1g; Sugar: 2g; Protein: 25g; Iron: 3mg; Sodium: 1182mg

Buffalo Chicken Wings

PREP: 5 MINUTES • COOK TIME: 30 MINUTES • TOTAL: 35 MINUTES • SERVES: 8

Ingredients

1 tsp. salt
1-2 tbsp. brown sugar
1 tbsp. Worcestershire sauce

½ C. vegan butter
½ C. cayenne pepper sauce
4 pounds chicken wings

Instructions:

1   Whisk salt, brown sugar, Worcestershire sauce, butter, and hot sauce together and set to the side. Dry wings and add to air fryer basket.

2   Set temperature to 380°F, and set time to 25 minutes. Cook tossing halfway through. When timer sounds, shake wings and bump up the temperature to 400 degrees and cook another 5 minutes.
Take out wings and place into a big bowl. Add sauce and toss well.
Serve alongside celery sticks.

Perfect Chicken Parmesan

PREP: 5 MINUTES • COOK TIME: 25 MINUTES • TOTAL: 30 MINUTES • SERVES: 2

Ingredients

2 large white meat chicken breasts
1 cup of breadcrumbs
2 medium-sized eggs
Pinch of salt and pepper

1 tablespoon of dried oregano
1 cup of marinara sauce
2 slices of provolone cheese
1 tablespoon of parmesan cheese

Instructions:

1. Cover the basket of the Air fryer with a lining of tin foil, leaving the edges uncovered to allow air to circulate through the basket.
Preheat the Salter air fryer to 350 degrees. In a mixing bowl, beat the eggs until fluffy and until the yolks and whites are fully combined, and set aside.
In a separate mixing bowl, combine the breadcrumbs, oregano, salt and pepper, and set aside. One by one, dip the raw chicken breasts into the bowl with dry ingredients, coating both sides; then submerge into the bowl with wet ingredients, then dip again into the dry ingredients. This double coating will ensure an extra crisp-and-delicious air-fry.
Lay the coated chicken breasts on the foil covering the Air fryer basket, in a single flat layer.

2.   Set the Salter air fryer timer for 10 minutes.
After 10 minutes, the air fryer will turn off and the chicken should be mid-way cooked and the breaded coating starting to brown.
Using tongs, turn each piece of chicken over to ensure a full all-over fry.
ReSet the Salter air fryer to 320 degrees for another 10 minutes.
While the chicken is cooking, pour half the marinara sauce into a 7-inch heat-safe pan.
After 15 minutes, when the air fryer shuts off, remove the fried chicken breasts using tongs and set in the marinara-covered pan. Drizzle the rest of the marinara sauce over the fried chicken, then place the slices of provolone cheese atop both of them and sprinkle the parmesan cheese over the entire pan.
ReSet the Salter air fryer to 350 degrees for 5 minutes.
After 5 minutes, when the air fryer shuts off, remove the dish from the air fryer using tongs or oven mitts. The chicken will be perfectly crisped and the cheese melted and lightly toasted. Serve while hot!

Air Fryer Grilled Chicken Breasts
PREP: 5 MINUTES • COOK TIME: 14 MINUTES • TOTAL: 19 MINUTES • SERVES: 4

Ingredients

½ teaspoon garlic powder

1 teaspoon salt

½ teaspoon freshly ground black pepper

1 teaspoon dried parsley

2 tablespoons olive oil, divided

3 boneless, skinless chicken breasts

Instructions:

1   In a small mixing bowl, mix together the garlic powder, salt, pepper, and parsley. Using 1 tablespoon of olive oil and half of the seasoning mix, rub each chicken breast with oil and seasonings. Place the chicken breast in the air fryer basket.

2   Set the temperature of your Salter AF to 370°F. Set the timer and grill for 7 minutes.
    Using tongs, flip the chicken and brush the remaining olive oil and spices onto the chicken. Reset the timer and grill for 7 minutes more. Check that the chicken has reached an internal temperature of 165°F. Add cooking time if needed.
    Once the chicken is fully cooked, transfer it to a platter and serve.

Per Serving: Calories: 182; Fat: 9g; Saturated fat: 1g; Carbohydrate: 0g; Fiber: 0g; Sugar: 0g; Protein: 26g; Iron: 1mg; Sodium: 657mg

Zingy & Nutty Chicken Wings
PREP: 5 MINUTES • COOK TIME: 18 MINUTES • TOTAL: 23 MINUTES • SERVES: 4

Ingredients

1 tablespoon fish sauce

1 tablespoon fresh lemon juice

1 teaspoon sugar

12 chicken middle wings, cut into half

2 fresh lemongrass stalks, chopped finely

¼ cup unsalted cashews, crushed

Instructions:

1. In a bowl, mix together fish sauce, lime juice and sugar.
    Add wings ad coat with mixture generously. Refrigerate to marinate for about 1-2 hours.
    Preheat the Salter air fryer to 355 degrees F.

2. In the Air fryer pan, place lemongrass stalks. Cook for about 2-3 minutes. Remove the cashew mixture from Air fryer and transfer into a bowl. Now, Set the Salter air fryer to 390 degrees F.
    Place the chicken wings in Air fryer pan. Cook for about 13-15 minutes further.
    Transfer the wings into serving plates. Sprinkle with cashew mixture and serve.

Pesto-Cream Chicken with Cherry Tomatoes
PREP: 10 MINUTES • COOK TIME: 15 MINUTES • TOTAL: 25 MINUTES • SERVES: 4

Ingredients

Vegetable oil spray

½ cup prepared pesto

¼ cup half-and-half

¼ grated Parmesan cheese

½ to 1 teaspoon red pepper flakes

1 pound boneless, skinless chicken thighs, halved crosswise

1 small onion, sliced

½cup sliced red and/or green bell peppers

½ cup halved cherry tomatoes

Instructions:

1   Spray a 6 × 3-inch round heatproof pan with vegetable oil spray; set aside. In a large bowl, combine the pesto, half-and-half, cheese, and red pepper flakes. Whisk until well combined. Add the chicken and turn to coat. Transfer the sauce and chicken to the prepared pan. Scatter the onion, bell pepper, and tomatoes on top.

2   Place the pan in the air fryer basket. Set the Salter air fryer to 350°F for 15 minutes. Use a meat thermometer to ensure the chicken has reached an internal temperature of 165°F.

Peanut Chicken

PREP: 15 MINUTES PLUS 30 MINUTES TO MARINATE • COOK TIME: 20 MINUTES • TOTAL: 1 HOUR 5 MINUTES • SERVES: 4

Ingredients

¼ cup creamy peanut butter
2 tablespoons sweet chili sauce
2 tablespoons fresh lime juice
1 tablespoon sriracha
1 tablespoon soy sauce
1 teaspoon minced fresh ginger
1 clove garlic, minced

½ teaspoon kosher salt
½ cup hot water
1 pound bone-in chicken thighs
2 tablespoons chopped fresh cilantro, for garnish
¼ cup chopped green onions, for garnish
2 to 3 tablespoons crushed roasted and salted peanuts, for garnish

Instructions:

1 In a small bowl, combine the peanut butter, sweet chili sauce, lime juice, sriracha, soy sauce, ginger, garlic, and salt. Add the hot water and whisk until smooth. Place the chicken in a resealable plastic bag and pour in half of the sauce. Reserve the remaining sauce for serving. Seal the bag and massage until all of the chicken is well coated. Marinate at room temperature for 30 minutes or in the refrigerator for up to 24 hours. Remove the chicken from the bag and discard the marinade. Place the chicken in the air fryer basket.

2 Set the Salter air fryer to 350°F for 20 minutes. Use a meat thermometer to ensure the chicken has reached an internal temperature of 165°F. Transfer the chicken to a serving platter. Sprinkle with the cilantro, green onions, and peanuts. Serve with the reserved sauce for dipping.

Basil-Garlic Breaded Chicken Bake

PREP: 5 MINUTES • COOK TIME: 25 MINUTES • TOTAL: 30 MINUTES • SERVES: 2

Ingredients

2 boneless skinless chicken breast halves
1 tablespoon butter, melted
1 large tomato, seeded and chopped
2 garlic cloves, minced
1 1/2 tablespoons minced fresh basil
1/2 tablespoon olive oil

1/2 teaspoon salt
1/4 cup all-purpose flour
1/4 cup egg substitute
1/4 cup grated Parmesan cheese
1/4 cup dry bread crumbs
1/4 teaspoon pepper

Instructions:

1 In shallow bowl, whisk well egg substitute and place flour in a separate bowl. Dip chicken in flour, then egg, and then flour. In small bowl whisk well butter, bread crumbs and cheese. Sprinkle over chicken. Lightly grease baking pan of air fryer with cooking spray. Place breaded chicken on bottom of pan. Cover with foil.

2 For 20 minutes, cook on 390°F.
Meanwhile, in a bowl whisk well remaining ingredient. Remove foil from pan and then pour over chicken the remaining Ingredients. Cook for 8 minutes. Serve and enjoy.

Per Serving: Calories: 311; Fat: 11g; Protein:31g; Carbs:22g

Pork Recipes

Pork Taquitos

PREP: 10 MINUTES • COOK TIME: 16 MINUTES • TOTAL: 26 MINUTES • SERVES: 8

Ingredients

1 juiced lime
10 whole wheat tortillas

2 ½ C. shredded mozzarella cheese
30 ounces of cooked and shredded pork tenderloin

Instructions:

1. Ensure your air fryer is preheated to 380 degrees.
    Drizzle pork with lime juice and gently mix.
    Heat up tortillas in the microwave with a dampened paper towel to soften.
    Add about 3 ounces of pork and ¼ cup of shredded cheese to each tortilla. Tightly roll them up.
    Spray the Salter air fryer basket with a bit of olive oil.
2. Set temperature to 380°F, and set time to 10 minutes. Air fry taquitos 7-10 minutes till tortillas turn a slight golden color, making sure to flip halfway through cooking process.

Per Serving: Calories: 309; Fat: 11g; Protein:21g; Sugar:2g

Cajun Bacon Pork Loin Fillet

PREP: 10 MINUTES PLUS 1 HOUR TO MARINATE•COOK TIME: 20 MINUTES•TOTAL:1 HOUR 30MINUTES•SERVES: 6

Ingredients

1½ pounds pork loin fillet or pork tenderloin
3 tablespoons olive oil
2 tablespoons Cajun Spice Mix

Salt
6 slices bacon
Olive oil spray

Instructions:

1. Cut the pork in half so that it will fit in the air fryer basket.
    Place both pieces of meat in a resealable plastic bag. Add the oil, Cajun seasoning, and salt to taste, if using. Seal the bag and massage to coat all of the meat with the oil and seasonings. Marinate in the refrigerator for at least 1 hour or up to 24 hours.
2. Remove the pork from the bag and wrap 3 bacon slices around each piece. Spray the Salter air fryer basket with olive oil spray. Place the meat in the air fryer. Set the Salter air fryer to 350°F for 15 minutes. Increase the temperature to 400°F for 5 minutes. Use a meat thermometer to ensure the meat has reached an internal temperature of 145°F.
    Let the meat rest for 10 minutes. Slice into 6 medallions and serve.

Panko-Breaded Pork Chops

PREP: 5 MINUTES • COOK TIME: 12 MINUTES • TOTAL: 17 MINUTES • SERVES: 6

Ingredients

5 (3½- to 5-ounce) pork chops (bone-in or boneless)
Seasoning salt
Pepper

¼ cup all-purpose flour
2 tablespoons panko bread crumbs
Cooking oil

Instructions:

1. Season the pork chops with the seasoning salt and pepper to taste.
   Sprinkle the flour on both sides of the pork chops, then coat both sides with panko bread crumbs.
   Place the pork chops in the air fryer. Stacking them is okay.
2. Spray the pork chops with cooking oil. Cook for 6 minutes.
   Open the Air fryer and flip the pork chops. Cook for an additional 6 minutes
   Cool before serving.
   Typically, bone-in pork chops are juicier than boneless. If you prefer really juicy pork chops, use bone-in.

Per Serving: Calories: 246; Fat: 13g; Protein:26g; Fiber:0g

Porchetta-Style Pork Chops

PREP: 10 MINUTES • COOK TIME: 15 MINUTES • TOTAL: 25 MINUTES • SERVES: 2

Ingredients

1 tablespoon extra-virgin olive oil
Grated zest of 1 lemon
2 cloves garlic, minced
2 teaspoons chopped fresh rosemary
1 teaspoon finely chopped fresh sage
1 teaspoon fennel seeds, lightly crushed

¼ to ½ teaspoon red pepper flakes
1 teaspoon kosher salt
1 teaspoon black pepper
(8-ounce) center-cut bone-in pork chops, about 1 inch thick

Instructions:

1. In a small bowl, combine the olive oil, zest, garlic, rosemary, sage, fennel seeds, red pepper, salt, and black pepper. Stir, crushing the herbs with the back of a spoon, until a paste forms. Spread the seasoning mix on both sides of the pork chops.
2. Place the chops in the air fryer basket. Set the Salter air fryer to 375°F for 15 minutes. Use a meat thermometer to ensure the chops have reached an internal temperature of 145°F.

Apricot Glazed Pork Tenderloins

PREP: 5 MINUTES • COOK TIME: 30 MINUTES • TOTAL: 35 MINUTES • SERVES: 3

Ingredients

1 teaspoon salt
1/2 teaspoon pepper
1-lb pork tenderloin
2 tablespoons minced fresh rosemary or 1 tablespoon dried rosemary, crushed
2 tablespoons olive oil, divided

1 garlic cloves, minced
Apricot Glaze Ingredients
1 cup apricot preserves
3 garlic cloves, minced
4 tablespoons lemon juice

Instructions:

1. Mix well pepper, salt, garlic, oil, and rosemary. Brush all over pork. If needed cut pork crosswise in half to fit in air fryer. Lightly grease baking pan of air fryer with cooking spray. Add pork.
2. For 3 minutes per side, brown pork in a preheated 390°F air fryer.Meanwhile, mix well all glaze Ingredients in a small bowl. Baste pork every 5 minutes. Cook for 20 minutes at 330°F. Serve and enjoy.

Sweet & Spicy Country-Style Ribs
PREP: 10 MINUTES • COOK TIME: 25 MINUTES • TOTAL: 35 MINUTES • SERVES: 4

Ingredients

2 tablespoons brown sugar
2 tablespoons smoked paprika
1 teaspoon garlic powder
1 teaspoon onion powder
1 teaspoon dry mustard
1 teaspoon ground cumin

1 teaspoon kosher salt
1 teaspoon black pepper
¼ to ½ teaspoon cayenne pepper
1½ pounds boneless country-style pork ribs
1 cup barbecue sauce

Instructions:

1. In a small bowl, stir together the brown sugar, paprika, garlic powder, onion powder, dry mustard, cumin, salt, black pepper, and cayenne. Mix until well combined.
   Pat the ribs dry with a paper towel. Generously sprinkle the rub evenly over both sides of the ribs and rub in with your fingers.
2. Place the ribs in the air fryer basket. Set the Salter air fryer to 350°F for 15 minutes. Turn the ribs and brush with ½ cup of the barbecue sauce. Cook for an additional 10 minutes. Use a meat thermometer to ensure the pork has reached an internal temperature of 145°F. Serve with remaining barbecue sauce.

Pork Tenders With Bell Peppers
PREP: 5 MINUTES • COOK TIME: 15 MINUTES • TOTAL: 20 MINUTES • SERVES: 4

Ingredients

11 Ozs Pork Tenderloin
1 Bell Pepper, in thin strips
1 Red Onion, sliced
2 Tsps Provencal Herbs

Black Pepper to taste
1 Tbsp Olive Oil
1/2 Tbsp Mustard

Instructions:

1. Preheat the Salter air fryer to 390 degrees.
   In the oven dish, mix the bell pepper strips with the onion, herbs, and some salt and pepper to taste.
   Add half a tablespoon of olive oil to the mixture
   Cut the pork tenderloin into four pieces and rub with salt, pepper and mustard.
   Thinly coat the pieces with remaining olive oil and place them upright in the oven dish on top of the pepper mixture
2. Place the bowl into the Air fryer. Set the timer to 15 minutes and roast the meat and the vegetables
   Turn the meat and mix the peppers halfway through
   Serve with a fresh salad

Wonton Meatballs
PREP: 15 MINUTES • COOK TIME: 10 MINUTES • TOTAL: 25 MINUTES • SERVES: 4

Ingredients
1 pound ground pork

2 large eggs

¼ cup chopped green onions (white and green parts)

¼ cup chopped fresh cilantro or parsley

1 tablespoon minced fresh ginger

3 cloves garlic, minced

2 teaspoons soy sauce

1 teaspoon oyster sauce

½ teaspoon kosher salt

1 teaspoon black pepper

Instructions:
1. In the bowl of a stand mixer fitted with the paddle attachment, combine the pork, eggs, green onions, cilantro, ginger, garlic, soy sauce, oyster sauce, salt, and pepper. Mix on low speed until all of the ingredients are incorporated, 2 to 3 minutes.
   Form the mixture into 12 meatballs and arrange in a single layer in the air fryer basket.
2. Set the Salter air fryer to 350°F for 10 minutes. Use a meat thermometer to ensure the meatballs have reached an internal temperature of 145°F.
   Transfer the meatballs to a bowl and serve.

Barbecue Flavored Pork Ribs
PREP: 5 MINUTES • COOK TIME: 15 MINUTES • TOTAL: 25 MINUTES • SERVES: 6

Ingredients
¼ cup honey, divided

¾ cup BBQ sauce

2 tablespoons tomato ketchup

1 tablespoon Worcestershire sauce

1 tablespoon soy sauce

½ teaspoon garlic powder

Freshly ground white pepper, to taste

1¾ pound pork ribs

Instructions:
1. In a large bowl, mix together 3 tablespoons of honey and remaining ingredients except pork ribs. Refrigerate to marinate for about 20 minutes. Preheat the Salter air fryer to 355 degrees F. Place the ribs in an Air fryer basket.
2. Cook for about 13 minutes. Remove the ribs from the Air fryer and coat with remaining honey. Serve hot.

Easy Air Fryer Marinated Pork Tenderloin
PREP:10 MINUTES PLUS 1HOUR TO MARINATE•COOK TIME:30 MINUTES•TOTAL:1 HOUR 40 MINUTES•SERVES:4-6

Ingredients
¼ cup olive oil

¼ cup soy sauce

¼ cup freshly squeezed lemon juice

1 garlic clove, minced

1 tablespoon Dijon mustard

1 teaspoon salt

½ teaspoon freshly ground black pepper

2 pounds pork tenderloin

Instructions:
1. In a large mixing bowl, make the marinade. Mix together the olive oil, soy sauce, lemon juice, minced garlic, Dijon mustard, salt, and pepper. Reserve ¼ cup of the marinade.
   Place the tenderloin in a large bowl and pour the remaining marinade over the meat. Cover and marinate in the refrigerator for about 1 hour. Place the marinated pork tenderloin into the air fryer basket.
2. Set the temperature of your Salter AF to 400°F. Set the timer and roast for 10 minutes. Using tongs, flip the pork and baste it with half of the reserved marinade. Reset the timer and roast for 10 minutes more.
   Using tongs, flip the pork, then baste with the remaining marinade.
   Reset the timer and roast for another 10 minutes, for a total cooking time of 30 minutes.

Balsamic Glazed Pork Chops

PREP: 5 MINUTES • COOK TIME: 50 MINUTES • TOTAL: 55 MINUTES • SERVES: 4

Ingredients

¾ cup balsamic vinegar
1 ½ tablespoons sugar
1 tablespoon butter

3 tablespoons olive oil
3 tablespoons salt
3 pork rib chops

Instructions:

1   Place all ingredients in bowl and allow the meat to marinate in the fridge for at least 2 hours. Preheat the Salter air fryer to 390°F. Place the grill pan accessory in the air fryer.

2   Grill the pork chops for 20 minutes making sure to flip the meat every 10 minutes for even grilling. Meanwhile, pour the balsamic vinegar on a saucepan and allow to simmer for at least 10 minutes until the sauce thickens.Brush the meat with the glaze before serving.

Per Serving: Calories: 274; Fat: 18g; Protein:17g

Perfect Air Fried Pork Chops

PREP: 5 MINUTES • COOK TIME: 17 MINUTES • TOTAL: 22 MINUTES • SERVES: 4

Ingredients

3 cups bread crumbs
½ cup grated Parmesan cheese
2 tablespoons vegetable oil
2 teaspoons salt

2 teaspoons sweet paprika
½ teaspoon onion powder
¼ teaspoon garlic powder
6 (½-inch-thick) bone-in pork chops

Instructions:

1   Spray the Salter air fryer basket with olive oil. In a large resealable bag, combine the bread crumbs, Parmesan cheese, oil, salt, paprika, onion powder, and garlic powder. Seal the bag and shake it a few times in order for the spices to blend together. Place the pork chops, one by one, in the bag and shake to coat.

2   Place the pork chops in the greased Salter air fryer basket in a single layer. Be careful not to overcrowd the basket. Spray the chops generously with olive oil to avoid powdery, uncooked breading.
Set the temperature of your Salter AF to 360°F. Set the timer and roast for 10 minutes.
Using tongs, flip the chops. Spray them generously with olive oil.
Reset the timer and roast for 7 minutes more.
Check that the pork has reached an internal temperature of 145°F. Add cooking time if needed.

Per Serving: Calories: 513; Fat: 23g; Saturated fat: 8g; Carbohydrate: 22g; Fiber: 2g; Sugar: 3g; Protein: 50g; Iron: 3mg; Sodium: 1521mg

Rustic Pork Ribs

PREP: 5 MINUTES • COOK TIME: 15 MINUTES • TOTAL: 25 MINUTES • SERVES: 4

Ingredients

1 rack of pork ribs
3 tablespoons dry red wine
1 tablespoon soy sauce
1/2 teaspoon dried thyme
1/2 teaspoon onion powder

1/2 teaspoon garlic powder
1/2 teaspoon ground black pepper
1 teaspoon smoke salt
1 tablespoon cornstarch
1/2 teaspoon olive oil

Instructions:

1.   Begin by preheating your Air fryer to 390 degrees F. Place all ingredients in a mixing bowl and let them marinate at least 1 hour.

2.   Cook the marinated ribs approximately 25 minutes at 390 degrees F. Serve hot.

Air Fryer Baby Back Ribs

PREP: 5 MINUTES • COOK TIME: 25 MINUTES • TOTAL: 30 MINUTES • SERVES: 4

Ingredients
1 rack baby back ribs
1 tablespoon garlic powder
1 teaspoon freshly ground black pepper

2 tablespoons salt
1 cup barbecue sauce (any type)

Instructions:
1. Dry the ribs with a paper towel.
   Season the ribs with the garlic powder, pepper, and salt.
   Place the seasoned ribs into the air fryer.
2. Set the temperature of your Salter AF to 400°F. Set the timer and grill for 10 minutes.
   Using tongs, flip the ribs.
   Reset the timer and grill for another 10 minutes.
   Once the ribs are cooked, use a pastry brush to brush on the barbecue sauce, then set the timer and grill for a final 3 to 5 minutes.

Per Serving: Calories: 422; Fat: 27g; Saturated fat: 10g; Carbohydrate: 25g; Fiber: 1g; Sugar: 17g; Protein: 18g; Iron: 1mg; Sodium: 4273mg

Keto Parmesan Crusted Pork Chops

PREP: 10 MINUTES • COOK TIME: 15 MINUTES • TOTAL: 25 MINUTES • SERVES: 8

Ingredients
3 tbsp. grated parmesan cheese
1 C. pork rind crumbs
2 beaten eggs
¼ tsp. chili powder
½ tsp. onion powder

1 tsp. smoked paprika
¼ tsp. pepper
½ tsp. salt
4-6 thick boneless pork chops

Instructions:
1. Ensure your air fryer is preheated to 400 degrees.
   With pepper and salt, season both sides of pork chops.
   In a food processor, pulse pork rinds into crumbs. Mix crumbs with other seasonings. Beat eggs and add to another bowl.
   Dip pork chops into eggs then into pork rind crumb mixture.
2. Spray down air fryer with olive oil and add pork chops to the basket. Set temperature to 400°F, and set time to 15 minutes.

Per Serving: Calories: 422; Fat: 19g; Protein:38g; Sugar:2g

Pork Milanese
PREP: 10 MINUTES • COOK TIME: 12 MINUTES • TOTAL: 22 MINUTES • SERVES: 4

Ingredients
4 (1-inch) boneless pork chops
Fine sea salt and ground black pepper
2 large eggs

¾ cup powdered Parmesan cheese about 2¼ ounces
Chopped fresh parsley, for garnish
Lemon slices, for serving

Instructions:
1. Spray the Salter air fryer basket with avocado oil. Preheat the Salter air fryer to 400°F. Place the pork chops between 2 sheets of plastic wrap and pound them with the flat side of a meat tenderizer until they're ¼ inch thick. Lightly season both sides of the chops with salt and pepper. Lightly beat the eggs in a shallow bowl. Divide the Parmesan cheese evenly between 2 bowls and set the bowls in this order: Parmesan, eggs, Parmesan. Dredge a chop in the first bowl of Parmesan, then dip it in the eggs, and then dredge it again in the second bowl of Parmesan, making sure both sides and all edges are well coated. Repeat with the remaining chops.
2. Place the chops in the Salter air fryer basket and cook for 12 minutes, or until the internal temperature reaches 145°F, flipping halfway through.
   Garnish with fresh parsley and serve immediately with lemon slices. Store leftovers in an airtight container in the refrigerator for up to 3 days. Reheat in a preheated 390°F air fryer for 5 minutes, or until warmed through.

Per serving: Calories **351**; Fat **18g**; Protein **42g**; Total carbs **3g**; Fiber **1g**

Crispy Fried Pork Chops the Southern Way
PREP: 10 MINUTES • COOK TIME: 25 MINUTES • TOTAL: 35 MINUTES • SERVES: 4

Ingredients
½ cup all-purpose flour
½ cup low fat buttermilk
½ teaspoon black pepper

½ teaspoon Tabasco sauce
teaspoon paprika
3 bone-in pork chops

Instructions:
1 Place the buttermilk and hot sauce in a Ziploc bag and add the pork chops. Allow to marinate for at least an hour in the fridge.
   In a bowl, combine the flour, paprika, and black pepper.
   Remove pork from the Ziploc bag and dredge in the flour mixture.
   Preheat the Salter air fryer to 390°F.
   Spray the pork chops with cooking oil.
2 Place in the Salter air fryer basket and cook for 25 minutes.

Per Serving: Calories: 427; Fat: 21.2g; Protein:46.4g; Sugar:2g

Italian Sausages with Peppers and Onions
PREP: 5 MINUTES • COOK TIME: 28 MINUTES • TOTAL: 33 MINUTES • SERVES: 3

Ingredients

1 medium onion, thinly sliced
1 yellow or orange bell pepper, thinly sliced
1 red bell pepper, thinly sliced
¼ cup avocado oil or melted coconut oil

1 teaspoon fine sea salt
6 Italian sausages
Dijon mustard, for serving (optional)

Instructions:

1   Preheat the Salter air fryer to 400°F. Place the onion and peppers in a large bowl. Drizzle with the oil and toss well to coat the veggies. Season with the salt.
Place the onion and peppers in a 6-inch pie pan and cook in the air fryer for 8 minutes, stirring halfway through. Remove from the air fryer and set aside.

2   Spray the Salter air fryer basket with avocado oil. Place the sausages in the Salter air fryer basket and cook for 20 minutes, or until crispy and golden brown. During the last minute or two of cooking, add the onion and peppers to the basket with the sausages to warm them through.
Place the onion and peppers on a serving platter and arrange the sausages on top. Serve Dijon mustard on the side, if desired.
Store leftovers in an airtight container in the fridge for up to 7 days or in the freezer for up to a month. Reheat in a preheated 390°F air fryer for 3 minutes, or until heated through.

Per serving: Calories 576; Fat 49g; Protein 25g; Total carbs 8g; Fiber 2g

Fried Pork Quesadilla
PREP: 10 MINUTES • COOK TIME: 12 MINUTES • TOTAL: 22 MINUTES • SERVES: 2

Ingredients

Two 6-inch corn or flour tortilla shells
1 medium-sized pork shoulder, approximately 4 ounces, sliced
½ medium-sized white onion, sliced
½ medium-sized red pepper, sliced

½ medium sized green pepper, sliced
½ medium sized yellow pepper, sliced
¼ cup of shredded pepper-jack cheese
¼ cup of shredded mozzarella cheese

Instructions:

1   Preheat the Salter air fryer to 350 degrees.
In the oven on high heat for 20 minutes, grill the pork, onion, and peppers in foil in the same pan, allowing the moisture from the vegetables and the juice from the pork mingle together. Remove pork and vegetables in foil from the oven. While they're cooling, sprinkle half the shredded cheese over one of the tortillas, then cover with the pieces of pork, onions, and peppers, and then layer on the rest of the shredded cheese. Top with the second tortilla. Place directly on hot surface of the Air fryer basket.

2   Set the Salter air fryer timer for 6 minutes. After 6 minutes, when the Air fryer shuts off, flip the tortillas onto the other side with a spatula; the cheese should be melted enough that it won't fall apart, but be careful anyway not to spill any toppings!
ReSet the Salter air fryer to 350 degrees for another 6 minutes.
After 6 minutes, when the air fryer shuts off, the tortillas should be browned and crisp, and the pork, onion, peppers and cheese will be crispy and hot and delicious. Remove with tongs and let sit on a serving plate to cool for a few minutes before slicing.

Cilantro-Mint Pork BBQ Thai Style
PREP: 5 MINUTES • COOK TIME: 15 MINUTES • TOTAL: 20 MINUTES • SERVES: 3

Ingredients

1 minced hot chile
1 minced shallot
1-pound ground pork
2 tablespoons fish sauce

2 tablespoons lime juice
3 tablespoons basil
3 tablespoons chopped mint
3 tablespoons cilantro

Instructions:

1   In a shallow dish, mix well all Ingredients with hands. Form into 1-inch ovals. Thread ovals in skewers. Place on skewer rack in air fryer.

2   For 15 minutes, cook on 360°F. Halfway through cooking time, turnover skewers. If needed, cook in batches. Serve and enjoy.

Per Serving: Calories: 455; Fat: 31.5g; Protein:40.4g

Pork Wonton Wonderful
PREP: 10 MINUTES • COOK TIME: 25 MINUTES • TOTAL: 35 MINUTES • SERVES: 3

Ingredients

8 wanton wrappers
4 ounces of raw minced pork
1 medium-sized green apple
1 cup of water, for wetting the wanton wrappers

1 tablespoon of vegetable oil
½ tablespoon of oyster sauce
1 tablespoon of soy sauce
Large pinch of ground white pepper

Instructions:

1   Cover the basket of the Air fryer with a lining of tin foil, leaving the edges uncovered to allow air to circulate through the basket. Preheat the Salter air fryer to 350 degrees. In a small mixing bowl, combine the oyster sauce, soy sauce, and white pepper, then add in the minced pork and stir thoroughly. Cover and set in the fridge to marinate for at least 15 minutes. Core the apple, and slice into small cubes – smaller than bite-sized chunks. Add the apples to the marinating meat mixture, and combine thoroughly. Spread the wonton wrappers, and fill each with a large spoonful of the filling. Wrap the wontons into triangles, so that the wrappers fully cover the filling, and seal with a drop of the water. Coat each filled and wrapped wonton thoroughly with the vegetable oil, to help ensure a nice crispy fry. Place the wontons on the foil-lined air-fryer basket.

2   Set the Salter air fryer timer to 25 minutes. Halfway through cooking time, shake the handle of the Salter air fryer basket vigorously to jostle the wontons and ensure even frying. After 25 minutes, when the Air fryer shuts off, the wontons will be crispy golden-brown on the outside and juicy and delicious on the inside. Serve directly from the Salter air fryer basket and enjoy while hot.

Crispy Roast Garlic-Salt Pork
PREP: 5 MINUTES • COOK TIME: 45 MINUTES • TOTAL: 50 MINUTES • SERVES: 4

Ingredients

1 teaspoon Chinese five spice powder
1 teaspoon white pepper

2 pounds pork belly
2 teaspoons garlic salt

Instructions:

1   Preheat the Salter air fryer to 390°F.
Mix all the spices in a bowl to create the dry rub.
Score the skin of the pork belly with a knife and season the entire pork with the spice rub.

2   Place in the Salter air fryer basket and cook for 40 to 45 minutes until the skin is crispy.
Chop before serving.

Scotch Eggs

PREP: 10 MINUTES • COOK TIME: 15 MINUTES • TOTAL: 25 MINUTES • SERVES: 8

Ingredients

2 pounds ground pork or ground beef
2 teaspoons fine sea salt
½ teaspoon ground black pepper, plus more for garnish

8 large hard-boiled eggs, peeled
2 cups pork dust
Dijon mustard, for serving (optional)

Instructions:

Spray the Salter air fryer basket with avocado oil. Preheat the Salter air fryer to 400°F. Place the ground pork in a large bowl, add the salt and pepper, and use your hands to mix until seasoned throughout. Flatten about ¼ pound of ground pork in the palm of your hand and place a peeled egg in the center. Fold the pork completely around the egg. Repeat with the remaining eggs. Place the pork dust in a medium-sized bowl. One at a time, roll the ground pork–covered eggs in the pork dust and use your hands to press it into the eggs to form a nice crust.

Place the eggs in the Salter air fryer basket and spray them with avocado oil.

Cook the eggs for 15 minutes, or until the internal temperature of the pork reaches 145°F and the outside is golden brown. Garnish with ground black pepper and serve with Dijon mustard, if desired.

Store leftovers in an airtight container in the fridge for up to 7 days or in the freezer for up to a month. Reheat in a preheated 400°F air fryer for 3 minutes, or until heated through.

Per serving: Calories 447; Fat 34g; Protein 43g; Total carbs 0.5g; Fiber 0g

Italian Parmesan Breaded Pork Chops

PREP: 5 MINUTES • COOK TIME: 25 MINUTES • TOTAL: 30 MINUTES • SERVES: 5

Ingredients

5 (3½- to 5-ounce) pork chops (bone-in or boneless)
1 teaspoon Italian seasoning
Seasoning salt
Pepper

¼ cup all-purpose flour
2 tablespoons Italian bread crumbs
3 tablespoons finely grated Parmesan cheese
Cooking oil

Instructions:

1   Season the pork chops with the Italian seasoning and seasoning salt and pepper to taste. Sprinkle the flour on both sides of the pork chops, then coat both sides with the bread crumbs and Parmesan cheese.

2   Place the pork chops in the Air fryer. Stacking them is okay. Spray the pork chops with cooking oil. Cook for 6 minutes. Open the Air fryer and flip the pork chops. Cook for an additional 6 minutes. Cool before serving. Instead of seasoning salt, you can use either chicken or pork rub for additional flavor. You can find these rubs in the spice aisle of the grocery store.

Per Serving: Calories: 334; Fat: 7g; Protein:34g; Fiber:0g

Pork Tenderloin with Avocado Lime Sauce

PREP:10 MINUTES PLUS 2 HOURS TO MARINATE•COOK TIME:15 MINUTES•TOTAL: 2 HOURS 25MINUTES•
SERVES:4

Ingredients

MARINADE:
½ cup lime juice
Grated zest of 1 lime
2 teaspoons stevia glycerite, or ¼ teaspoon liquid stevia
3 cloves garlic, minced
1½ teaspoons fine sea salt
1 teaspoon chili powder, or more for more heat
1 teaspoon smoked paprika
1 pound pork tenderloin
AVOCADO LIME SAUCE:

1 medium-sized ripe avocado, roughly chopped
½ cup full-fat sour cream
Grated zest of 1 lime
Juice of 1 lime
2 cloves garlic, roughly chopped
½ teaspoon fine sea salt
¼ teaspoon ground black pepper
Chopped fresh cilantro leaves, for garnish
Lime slices, for serving
Pico de gallo, for serving

Instructions:

1 In a medium-sized casserole dish, stir together all the marinade ingredients until well combined. Add the tenderloin and coat it well in the marinade. Cover and place in the fridge to marinate for 2 hours or overnight. Spray the Salter air fryer basket with avocado oil. Preheat the Salter air fryer to 400°F.

2 Remove the pork from the marinade and place it in the air fryer basket. Cook for 13 to 15 minutes, until the internal temperature of the pork is 145°F, flipping after 7 minutes. Remove the pork from the air fryer and place it on a cutting board. Allow it to rest for 8 to 10 minutes, then cut it into ½-inch-thick slices.

   While the pork cooks, make the avocado lime sauce: Place all the sauce ingredients in a food processor and puree until smooth. Taste and adjust the seasoning to your liking.

   Place the pork slices on a serving platter and spoon the avocado lime sauce on top. Garnish with cilantro leaves and serve with lime slices and pico de gallo.

   Store leftovers in an airtight container in the fridge for up to 4 days. Reheat in a preheated 400°F air fryer for 5 minutes, or until heated through.

Per serving: Calories 326; Fat 19g; Protein 26g; Total carbs 15g; Fiber 6g

Beef recipes

Cheeseburger Egg Rolls
PREP: 10 MINUTES • COOK TIME: 7 MINUTES • TOTAL: 17 MINUTES • SERVES: 6

Ingredients

6 egg roll wrappers
6 chopped dill pickle chips
1 tbsp. yellow mustard
3 tbsp. cream cheese
3 tbsp. shredded cheddar cheese

½ C. chopped onion
½ C. chopped bell pepper
¼ tsp. onion powder
¼ tsp. garlic powder
8 ounces of raw lean ground beef

Instructions:

1 In a skillet, add seasonings, beef, onion, and bell pepper. Stir and crumble beef till fully cooked, and vegetables are soft. Take skillet off the heat and add cream cheese, mustard, and cheddar cheese, stirring till melted. Pour beef mixture into a bowl and fold in pickles.
Lay out egg wrappers and place 1/6th of beef mixture into each one. Moisten egg roll wrapper edges with water. Fold sides to the middle and seal with water. Repeat with all other egg rolls.
Place rolls into air fryer, one batch at a time.
2 Set temperature to 392°F, and set time to 7 minutes.

Per Serving: Calories: 153; Fat: 4g; Protein:12g; Sugar:3g

Air Fried Grilled Steak
PREP: 5 MINUTES • COOK TIME: 45 MINUTES • TOTAL: 50 MINUTES • SERVES: 2

Ingredients

2 top sirloin steaks
3 tablespoons butter, melted

3 tablespoons olive oil
Salt and pepper to taste

Instructions:

1 Preheat the Salter air fryer for 5 minutes. Season the sirloin steaks with olive oil, salt and pepper. Place the beef in the air fryer basket.
2 Cook for 45 minutes at 350°F. Once cooked, serve with butter.

Per Serving: Calories: 1536; Fat: 123.7g; Protein:103.4g

Beef Brisket Recipe from Texas
PREP: 15 MINUTES • COOK TIME: 1HOUR AND 30 MINUTES • SERVES: 8

Ingredients

1 ½ cup beef stock
1 bay leaf
1 tablespoon garlic powder
1 tablespoon onion powder
2 pounds beef brisket, trimmed

2 tablespoons chili powder
2 teaspoons dry mustard
4 tablespoons olive oil
Salt and pepper to taste

Instructions:

1 Preheat the Salter air fryer for 5 minutes. Place all ingredients in a deep baking dish that will fit in the air fryer.
2 Bake for 1 hour and 30 minutes at 400°F.
Stir the beef every after 30 minutes to soak in the sauce.

Per Serving: Calories: 306; Fat: 24.1g; Protein:18.3g

Savory Beefy Poppers

PREP: 15 MINUTES • COOK TIME: 15 MINUTES • TOTAL: 30 MINUTES • SERVES: 8

Ingredients

8 medium jalapeño peppers, stemmed, halved, and seeded
1 (8-ounce) package cream cheese softened
2 pounds ground beef (85% lean)

1 teaspoon fine sea salt
½ teaspoon ground black pepper
8 slices thin-cut bacon
Fresh cilantro leaves, for garnish

Instructions:

1. Spray the Salter air fryer basket with avocado oil. Preheat the Salter air fryer to 400°F. Stuff each jalapeño half with a few tablespoons of cream cheese. Place the halves back together again to form 8 jalapeños.
Season the ground beef with the salt and pepper and mix with your hands to incorporate. Flatten about ¼ pound of ground beef in the palm of your hand and place a stuffed jalapeño in the center. Fold the beef around the jalapeño, forming an egg shape. Wrap the beef-covered jalapeño with a slice of bacon and secure it with a toothpick.
2. Place the jalapeños in the air fryer basket, leaving space between them (if you're using a smaller air fryer, work in batches if necessary), and cook for 15 minutes, or until the beef is cooked through and the bacon is crispy. Garnish with cilantro before serving. Store leftovers in an airtight container in the fridge for 3 days or in the freezer for up to a month. Reheat in a preheated 350°F air fryer for 4 minutes, or until heated through and the bacon is crispy.

Per serving: Calories 679; Fat 53g; Protein 42g; Total carbs 3g; Fiber 1g

Juicy Cheeseburgers

PREP: 5 MINUTES • COOK TIME: 15 MINUTES • TOTAL: 20 MINUTES • SERVES: 4

Ingredients

1 pound 93% lean ground beef
1 teaspoon Worcestershire sauce
1 tablespoon burger seasoning
Salt

Pepper
Cooking oil
4 slices cheese
2 buns

Instructions:

1. In a large bowl, mix the ground beef, Worcestershire, burger seasoning, and salt and pepper to taste until well blended. Spray the Salter air fryer basket with cooking oil. You will need only a quick spritz. The burgers will produce oil as they cook. Shape the mixture into 4 patties. Place the burgers in the air fryer. The burgers should fit without the need to stack, but stacking is okay if necessary.
2. Cook for 8 minutes. Open the air fryer and flip the burgers. Cook for an additional 3 to 4 minutes. Check the inside of the burgers to determine if they have finished cooking. You can stick a knife or fork in the center to examine the color. Top each burger with a slice of cheese. Cook for an additional minute, or until the cheese has melted. Serve on buns with any additional toppings of your choice.

Per Serving: Calories: 566; Fat: 39g; Protein:29g; Fiber:1g

Copycat Taco Bell Crunch Wraps
PREP: 10 MINUTES • COOK TIME: 2 MINUTES • TOTAL: 15 MINUTES • SERVES: 6

Ingredients

6 wheat tostadas
2 C. sour cream
2 C. Mexican blend cheese
2 C. shredded lettuce
12 ounces low-sodium nacho cheese

3 Roma tomatoes
6 12-inch wheat tortillas
1 1/3 C. water
2 packets low-sodium taco seasoning
2 pounds of lean ground beef

Instructions:

1   Ensure your air fryer is preheated to 400 degrees.
Make beef according to taco seasoning packets.
Place 2/3 C. prepared beef, 4 tbsp. cheese, 1 tostada, 1/3 C. sour cream, 1/3 C. lettuce, 1/6th of tomatoes and 1/3 C. cheese on each tortilla.
Fold up tortillas edges and repeat with remaining ingredients.
Lay the folded sides of tortillas down into the air fryer and spray with olive oil.
2   Set temperature to 400°F, and set time to 2 minutes. Cook 2 minutes till browned.

Per Serving: Calories: 311; Fat: 9g; Protein:22g; Sugar:2g

Swedish Meatloaf
PREP: 10 MINUTES • COOK TIME: 35 MINUTES • TOTAL: 45 MINUTES • SERVES: 8

Ingredients

1½ pounds ground beef (85% lean)
¼ pound ground pork or ground beef
1 large egg (omit for egg-free)
½ cup minced onions
¼ cup tomato sauce
2 tablespoons dry mustard
2 cloves garlic, minced
2 teaspoons fine sea salt
1 teaspoon ground black pepper, plus more for garnish

SAUCE:
½ cup (1 stick) unsalted butter
½ cup shredded Swiss or mild cheddar cheese (about 2 ounces)
2 ounces cream cheese (¼ cup), softened
⅓ cup beef broth
⅛ teaspoon ground nutmeg
Halved cherry tomatoes, for serving (optional)

Instructions:

1. Preheat the Salter air fryer to 390°F.

In a large bowl, combine the ground beef, ground pork, egg, onions, tomato sauce, dry mustard, garlic, salt, and pepper. Using your hands, mix until well combined.

2. Place the meatloaf mixture in a 9 by 5-inch loaf pan and place it in the air fryer. Cook for 35 minutes, or until cooked through and the internal temperature reaches 145°F. Check the meatloaf after 25 minutes; if it's getting too brown on the top, cover it loosely with foil to prevent burning.

While the meatloaf cooks, make the sauce: Heat the butter in a saucepan over medium-high heat until it sizzles and brown flecks appear, stirring constantly to keep the butter from burning. Turn the heat down to low and whisk in the Swiss cheese, cream cheese, broth, and nutmeg. Simmer for at least 10 minutes. The longer it simmers, the more the flavors open up. When the meatloaf is done, transfer it to a serving tray and pour the sauce over it. Garnish with ground black pepper and serve with cherry tomatoes, if desired. Allow the meatloaf to rest for 10 minutes before slicing so it doesn't crumble apart.

Store leftovers in an airtight container in the fridge for 3 days or in the freezer for up to a month. Reheat in a preheated 350°F air fryer for 4 minutes, or until heated through.

Per serving: Calories 395; Fat 32g; Protein 23g; Total carbs 3g; Fiber 1g

Carne Asada

PREP: 5 MINUTES PLUS 2 HOURS TO MARINATE•COOK TIME: 8 MINUTES•TOTAL:2 HOURS 13 MINUTES•SERVES: 4

Ingredients

MARINADE:

1 cup fresh cilantro leaves and stems, plus more for garnish if desired

1 jalapeño pepper, seeded and diced

½ cup lime juice

2 tablespoons avocado oil

2 tablespoons coconut vinegar or apple cider vinegar

2 teaspoons orange extract

1 teaspoon stevia glycerite, or ⅛ teaspoon liquid stevia

2 teaspoons ancho chili powder

2 teaspoons fine sea salt

1 teaspoon coriander seeds

1 teaspoon cumin seeds

1pound skirt steak, cut into 4 equal portions

FOR SERVING (OPTIONAL):

Chopped avocado

Lime slices

Sliced radishes

Instructions:

1. Make the marinade: Place all the ingredients for the marinade in a blender and puree until smooth. Place the steak in a shallow dish and pour the marinade over it, making sure the meat is covered completely. Cover and place in the fridge for 2 hours or overnight.
   Spray the Salter air fryer basket with avocado oil. Preheat the Salter air fryer to 400°F.
2. Remove the steak from the marinade and place it in the Salter air fryer basket in one layer. Cook for 8 minutes, or until the internal temperature is 145°F; do not overcook or it will become tough.
   Remove the steak from the air fryer and place it on a cutting board to rest for 10 minutes before slicing it against the grain. Garnish with cilantro, if desired, and serve with chopped avocado, lime slices, and/or sliced radishes, if desired. Store leftovers in an airtight container in the fridge for 3 days or in the freezer for up to a month. Reheat in a preheated 350°F air fryer for 4 minutes, or until heated through.

Per serving: Calories 263; Fat 17g; Protein 24g; Total carbs 4g; Fiber 1g

Spicy Thai Beef Stir-Fry

PREP: 15 MINUTES • COOK TIME: 9 MINUTES • TOTAL: 24 MINUTES • SERVES: 4

Ingredients

1pound sirloin steaks, thinly sliced

2 tablespoons lime juice, divided

⅓ cup crunchy peanut butter

½ cup beef broth

1 tablespoon olive oil

1½ cups broccoli florets

2 cloves garlic, sliced

1 to 2 red chile peppers, sliced

Instructions:

1. In a medium bowl, combine the steak with 1 tablespoon of the lime juice. Set aside.
   Combine the peanut butter and beef broth in a small bowl and mix well. Drain the beef and add the juice from the bowl into the peanut butter mixture.
   In a 6-inch metal bowl, combine the olive oil, steak, and broccoli.
2. Cook for 3 to 4 minutes or until the steak is almost cooked and the broccoli is crisp and tender, shaking the basket once during cooking time.
   Add the garlic, chile peppers, and the peanut butter mixture and stir.
   Cook for 3 to 5 minutes or until the sauce is bubbling and the broccoli is tender.
   Serve over hot rice.

Per Serving: Calories: 387; Fat: 22g; Protein:42g; Fiber:2g

Air Fryer Beef Casserole
PREP: 5 MINUTES • COOK TIME: 30 MINUTES • TOTAL: 35 MINUTES • SERVES: 4

Ingredients
1 green bell pepper, seeded and chopped
1 onion, chopped
1-pound ground beef
3 cloves of garlic, minced

3 tablespoons olive oil
6 cups eggs, beaten
Salt and pepper to taste

Instructions:
1   Preheat the Salter air fryer for 5 minutes. In a baking dish that will fit in the air fryer, mix the ground beef, onion, garlic, olive oil, and bell pepper. Season with salt and pepper to taste.
    Pour in the beaten eggs and give a good stir. Place the dish with the beef and egg mixture in the air fryer.
2   Bake for 30 minutes at 325°F.

Per Serving: Calories: 1520; Fat: 125.11g; Protein:87.9g

Salisbury Steak with Mushroom Onion Gravy
PREP: 10 MINUTES • COOK TIME: 33 MINUTES • TOTAL: 43 MINUTES • SERVES: 2

Ingredients
MUSHROOM ONION GRAVY:
¾ cup sliced button mushrooms
¼ cup thinly sliced onions
¼ cup unsalted butter, melted (or bacon fat for dairy-free)
½ teaspoon fine sea salt
¼ cup beef broth
STEAKS:
½ pound ground beef (85% lean)

¼ cup minced onions, or ½ teaspoon onion powder
2 tablespoons tomato paste
1 tablespoon dry mustard
1 clove garlic, minced, or ¼ teaspoon garlic powder
½ teaspoon fine sea salt
¼ teaspoon ground black pepper, plus more for garnish if desired
Chopped fresh thyme leaves, for garnish (optional)

Instructions:
1. Preheat the Salter air fryer to 390°F.
    Make the gravy: Place the mushrooms and onions in a casserole dish that will fit in your air fryer. Pour the melted butter over them and stir to coat, then season with the salt. Place the dish in the air fryer and cook for 5 minutes, stir, then cook for another 3 minutes, or until the onions are soft and the mushrooms are browning. Add the broth and cook for another 10 minutes.
    While the gravy is cooking, prepare the steaks: In a large bowl, mix together the ground beef, onions, tomato paste, dry mustard, garlic, salt, and pepper until well combined. Form the mixture into 2 oval-shaped patties.
2. Place the patties on top of the mushroom gravy. Cook for 10 minutes, gently flip the patties, then cook for another 2 to 5 minutes, until the beef is cooked through and the internal temperature reaches 145°F.
    Transfer the steaks to a serving platter and pour the gravy over them. Garnish with ground black pepper and chopped fresh thyme, if desired. Store leftovers in an airtight container in the fridge for 3 days or in the freezer for up to a month. Reheat in a preheated 350°F air fryer for 4 minutes, or until heated through.

Per serving: Calories 588; Fat 44g; Protein 33g; Total carbs 11g; Fiber 3g

Fajita Meatball Lettuce Wraps
PREP: 10 MINUTES • COOK TIME: 10 MINUTES • TOTAL: 20 MINUTES • SERVES: 4

Ingredients

1 pound ground beef (85% lean)
½ cup salsa, plus more for serving if desired
¼ cup chopped onions
¼ cup diced green or red bell peppers
1 large egg, beaten
1 teaspoon fine sea salt
½ teaspoon chili powder

½ teaspoon ground cumin
1 clove garlic, minced
FOR SERVING (OPTIONAL):
8 leaves Boston lettuce
Pico de gallo or salsa
Lime slices

Instructions:

1. Spray the Salter air fryer basket with avocado oil. Preheat the Salter air fryer to 350°F. In a large bowl, mix together all the ingredients until well combined.
Shape the meat mixture into eight 1-inch balls.
2. Place the meatballs in the air fryer basket, leaving a little space between them. Cook for 10 minutes, or until cooked through and no longer pink inside and the internal temperature reaches 145°F. Serve each meatball on a lettuce leaf, topped with pico de gallo or salsa, if desired. Serve with lime slices if desired. Store leftovers in an airtight container in the fridge for 3 days or in the freezer for up to a month. Reheat in a preheated 350°F air fryer for 4 minutes, or until heated through.
Per serving: Calories 272; Fat 18g; Protein 23g; Total carbs 3g; Fiber 0.5g

Chimichurri Skirt Steak
PREP: 10 MINUTES • COOK TIME: 8 MINUTES • TOTAL: 18 MINUTES • SERVES: 2

Ingredients

2 x 8 oz Skirt Steak
1 cup Finely Chopped Parsley
¼ cup Finely Chopped Mint
2 Tbsp Fresh Oregano (Washed & finely chopped)
3 Finely Chopped Cloves of Garlic
1 Tsp Red Pepper Flakes (Crushed)
1 Tbsp Ground Cumin

1 Tsp Cayenne Pepper
2 Tsp Smoked Paprika
1 Tsp Salt
¼ Tsp Pepper
¾ cup Oil
3 Tbsp Red Wine Vinegar

Instructions:

1. Throw all the ingredients in a bowl (besides the steak) and mix well.
Put ¼ cup of the mixture in a plastic baggie with the steak and leave in the fridge overnight (2–24hrs).
2. Leave the bag out at room temperature for at least 30 min before popping into the Air fryer. Preheat for a minute or two to 390° F before cooking until med–rare (8–10 min).
Put 2 Tbsp of the chimichurri mix on top of each steak before serving.

Reuben Fritters

PREP: 10 MINUTES • COOK TIME: 16 MINUTES • TOTAL: 17 MINUTES • SERVES: 1 dozen fritters

Ingredients

2 cups finely diced cooked corned beef
1 (8-ounce) package cream cheese, softened
½ cup finely shredded Swiss cheese (about 2 ounces)
¼ cup sauerkraut

1 cup pork dust or powdered Parmesan cheese
Chopped fresh thyme, for garnish
Thousand Island Dipping Sauce for serving
Cornichons, for serving (optional)

Instructions:

1. Spray the Salter air fryer basket with avocado oil. Preheat the Salter air fryer to 390°F. In a large bowl, mix together the corned beef, cream cheese, Swiss cheese, and sauerkraut until well combined. Form the corned beef mixture into twelve 1½-inch balls.

   Place the pork dust in a shallow bowl. Roll the corned beef balls in the pork dust and use your hands to form it into a thick crust around each ball.

2. Place 6 balls in the air fryer basket, spaced about ½ inch apart, and cook for 8 minutes, or until golden brown and crispy. Allow them to cool a bit before lifting them out of the air fryer (the fritters are very soft when the cheese is melted; they're easier to handle once the cheese has hardened a bit). Repeat with the remaining fritters.

   Garnish with chopped fresh thyme and serve with the dipping sauce and cornichons, if desired. Store leftovers in an airtight container in the fridge for 3 days or in the freezer for up to a month. Reheat in a preheated 350°F air fryer for 4 minutes, or until heated through.

Per serving: Calories 527; Fat 50g; Protein 18g; Total carbs 2g; Fiber 0.1g

Charred Onions And Steak Cube BBQ

PREP: 5 MINUTES • COOK TIME: 40 MINUTES • TOTAL: 45 MINUTES • SERVES: 3

Ingredients

1 cup red onions, cut into wedges
1 tablespoon dry mustard
1 tablespoon olive oil

1-pound boneless beef sirloin, cut into cubes
Salt and pepper to taste

Instructions:

1. Preheat the Salter air fryer to 390°F.

   Place the grill pan accessory in the air fryer.

   Toss all ingredients in a bowl and mix until everything is coated with the seasonings.

2. Place on the grill pan and cook for 40 minutes.

   Halfway through the cooking time, give a stir to cook evenly.

Per Serving: Calories: 260; Fat: 10.7g; Protein:35.5g

Steak and Mushroom Gravy

PREP: 15 MINUTES • COOK TIME: 15 MINUTES • TOTAL: 30 MINUTES • SERVES: 4

Ingredients

4 cubed steaks
2 large eggs
1/2 dozen mushrooms
4 tablespoons unsalted butter
4 tablespoons black pepper
2 tablespoons salt
1/2 teaspoon onion powder

1/2 teaspoon garlic powder
1/4 teaspoon cayenne powder
1 1/4 teaspoons paprika
1 1/2 cups whole milk
1/3 cup flour
2 tablespoons vegetable oil

Instructions:

1   Mix 1/2 flour and a pinch of black pepper in a shallow bowl or on a plate. Beat 2 eggs in a bowl and mix in a pinch of salt and pepper.
In another shallow bowl mix together the other half of the flour with a pepper to taste, garlic powder, paprika, cayenne, and onion powder.
Chop mushrooms and set aside. Press your steak into the first flour bowl, then dip in egg, then press the steak into the second flour bowl until covered completely.

2   Cook steak in your Air fryer at 360 degrees for 15 Minutes, flipping halfway through. While the steak cooks, warm the butter over medium heat and add mushrooms to sauté. Add 4 tablespoons of the flour and pepper mix to the pan and mix until there are no clumps of flour. Mix in whole milk and simmer. Serve over steak for breakfast, lunch, or dinner.

Per Serving: Calories: 442; Fat: 27g; Protein:32g; Fiber:2.3g

Country Fried Steak

PREP: 5 MINUTES • COOK TIME: 12 MINUTES • TOTAL: 20 MINUTES • SERVES: 2

Ingredients

1 tsp. pepper
2 C. almond milk
2 tbsp. almond flour
6 ounces ground sausage meat
1 tsp. pepper
1 tsp. salt

1 tsp. garlic powder
1 tsp. onion powder
1 C. panko breadcrumbs
1 C. almond flour
3 beaten eggs
6 ounces sirloin steak, pounded till thin

Instructions:

1   Season panko breadcrumbs with spices. Dredge steak in flour, then egg, and then seasoned panko mixture. Place into air fryer basket.

2   Set temperature to 370°F, and set time to 12 minutes. To make sausage gravy, cook sausage and drain off fat, but reserve 2 tablespoons. Add flour to sausage and mix until incorporated. Gradually mix in milk over medium to high heat till it becomes thick. Season mixture with pepper and cook 3 minutes longer. Serve steak topped with gravy and enjoy.

Per Serving: Calories: 395; Fat: 11g; Protein:39g; Sugar:5g

Greek Stuffed Tenderloin

PREP: 10 MINUTES • COOK TIME: 10 MINUTES • TOTAL: 20 MINUTES • SERVES: 4

Ingredients

1½ pounds venison or beef tenderloin, pounded to ¼ inch thick
3 teaspoons fine sea salt
1 teaspoon ground black pepper
2 ounces creamy goat cheese
½ cup crumbled feta cheese (about 2 ounces)
¼ cup finely chopped onions

2 cloves garlic, minced
FOR GARNISH/SERVING (OPTIONAL):
Prepared yellow mustard
Halved cherry tomatoes
Extra-virgin olive oil
Sprigs of fresh rosemary
Lavender flowers

Instructions:

1. Spray the Salter air fryer basket with avocado oil. Preheat the Salter air fryer to 400°F. Season the tenderloin on all sides with the salt and pepper.
   In a medium-sized mixing bowl, combine the goat cheese, feta, onions, and garlic. Place the mixture in the center of the tenderloin. Starting at the end closest to you, tightly roll the tenderloin like a jelly roll. Tie the rolled tenderloin tightly with kitchen twine.

2. Place the meat in the Salter air fryer basket and cook for 5 minutes. Flip the meat over and cook for another 5 minutes, or until the internal temperature reaches 135°F for medium-rare. To serve, smear a line of prepared yellow mustard on a platter, then place the meat next to it and add halved cherry tomatoes on the side, if desired. Drizzle with olive oil and garnish with rosemary sprigs and lavender flowers, if desired.
   Best served fresh. Store leftovers in an airtight container in the fridge for 3 days. Reheat in a preheated 350°F air fryer for 4 minutes, or until heated through.

Per serving: Calories **415;** Fat **16g;** Protein **62g;** Total carbs **4g;** Fiber **0.3g**

Warming Winter Beef with Celery

PREP: 5 MINUTES • COOK TIME: 12 MINUTES • TOTAL: 15 MINUTES • SERVES: 4

Ingredients

9 ounces tender beef, chopped
1/2 cup leeks, chopped
1/2 cup celery stalks, chopped
2 cloves garlic, smashed
2 tablespoons red cooking wine

3/4 cup cream of celery soup
2 sprigs rosemary, chopped
1/4 teaspoon smoked paprika
3/4 teaspoons salt
1/4 teaspoon black pepper, or to taste

Instructions:

1 Add the beef, leeks, celery, and garlic to the baking dish; cook for about 5 minutes at 390 degrees F.
   Once the meat is starting to tender, pour in the wine and soup. Season with rosemary, smoked paprika, salt, and black pepper. Now, cook an additional 7 minutes.

Black and Blue Burgers

PREP: 5 MINUTES • COOK TIME:10 MINUTES • TOTAL: 15 MINUTES • SERVES: 2

Ingredients

½ teaspoon fine sea salt
¼ teaspoon ground black pepper
¼ teaspoon garlic powder
¼ teaspoon onion powder
¼ teaspoon smoked paprika
2 (¼-pound) hamburger patties, ½ inch thick

½ cup crumbled blue cheese (about 2 ounces)
2 Hamburger Buns
2 tablespoons mayonnaise
6 red onion slices
2 Boston lettuce leaves

Instructions:

1 Spray the Salter air fryer basket with avocado oil. Preheat the Salter air fryer to 360°F.In a small bowl, combine the salt, pepper, and seasonings. Season the patties well on both sides with the seasoning mixture.

2 Place the patties in the Salter air fryer basket and cook for 7 minutes, or until the internal temperature reaches 145°F for a medium-done burger. Place the blue cheese on top of the patties and cook for another minute to melt the cheese. Remove the burgers from the air fryer and allow to rest for 5 minutes. Slice the buns in half and smear 2 halves with a tablespoon of mayo each. Increase the heat to 400°F and place the buns in the Salter air fryer basket cut side up. Toast the buns for 1 to 2 minutes, until golden brown. Remove the buns from the air fryer and place them on a serving plate. Place the burgers on the buns and top each burger with 3 red onion slices and a lettuce leaf.

Per serving: Calories 237; Fat 20g; Protein 11g; Total carbs 3g; Fiber 1g

Cheesy Ground Beef And Mac Taco Casserole

PREP: 10 MINUTES • COOK TIME: 25 MINUTES • TOTAL: 35 MINUTES • SERVES: 5

Ingredients

1-ounce shredded Cheddar cheese
1-ounce shredded Monterey Jack cheese
2 tablespoons chopped green onions
1/2 (10.75 ounce) can condensed tomato soup
1/2-pound lean ground beef
1/2 cup crushed tortilla chips

1/4-pound macaroni, cooked according to manufacturer's Instructions
1/4 cup chopped onion
1/4 cup sour cream (optional)
1/2 (1.25 ounce) package taco seasoning mix
1/2 (14.5 ounce) can diced tomatoes

Instructions:

1 Lightly grease baking pan of air fryer with cooking spray. Add onion and ground beef. For 10 minutes, cook on 360°F. Halfway through cooking time, stir and crumble ground beef. Add taco seasoning, diced tomatoes, and tomato soup. Mix well. Mix in pasta. Sprinkle crushed tortilla chips. Sprinkle cheese.

2 Cook for 15 minutes at 390°F until tops are lightly browned and cheese is melted. Serve and enjoy.

Meat Lovers' Pizza
PREP: 10 MINUTES • COOK TIME: 12 MINUTES • TOTAL: 22 MINUTES • SERVES: 2

Ingredients

1 pre-prepared 7-inch pizza pie crust, defrosted if necessary.

1/3 cup of marinara sauce.

2 ounces of grilled steak, sliced into bite-sized pieces

2 ounces of salami, sliced fine

2 ounces of pepperoni, sliced fine

¼ cup of American cheese

¼ cup of shredded mozzarella cheese

Instructions:

1   Preheat the Salter air fryer to 350 degrees. Lay the pizza dough flat on a sheet of parchment paper or tin foil, cut large enough to hold the entire pie crust, but small enough that it will leave the edges of the air frying basket uncovered to allow for air circulation. Using a fork, stab the pizza dough several times across the surface – piercing the pie crust will allow air to circulate throughout the crust and ensure even cooking. With a deep soup spoon, ladle the marinara sauce onto the pizza dough, and spread evenly in expanding circles over the surface of the pie-crust. Be sure to leave at least ½ inch of bare dough around the edges, to ensure that extra-crispy crunchy first bite of the crust! Distribute the pieces of steak and the slices of salami and pepperoni evenly over the sauce-covered dough, then sprinkle the cheese in an even layer on top.

2   Set the Salter air fryer timer to 12 minutes, and place the pizza with foil or paper on the fryer's basket surface. Again, be sure to leave the edges of the basket uncovered to allow for proper air circulation, and don't let your bare fingers touch the hot surface. After 12 minutes, when the Air fryer shuts off, the cheese should be perfectly melted and lightly crisped, and the pie crust should be golden brown. Using a spatula – or two, if necessary, remove the pizza from the Salter air fryer basket and set on a serving plate. Wait a few minutes until the pie is cool enough to handle, then cut into slices and serve.

Mushroom and Swiss Burgers
PREP: 5 MINUTES • COOK TIME: 15 MINUTES • TOTAL: 20 MINUTES• SERVES: 2

Ingredients

2 large portobello mushrooms

1 teaspoon fine sea salt, divided

¼ teaspoon garlic powder

¼ teaspoon ground black pepper

¼ teaspoon onion powder

¼ teaspoon smoked paprika

2 (¼-pound) hamburger patties, ½ inch thick

2 slices Swiss cheese (omit for dairy-free)

Condiments of choice, such as Ranch Dressing, prepared yellow mustard, or mayonnaise, for serving

Instructions:

1   Preheat the Salter air fryer to 360°F. Clean the portobello mushrooms and remove the stems. Spray the mushrooms on all sides with avocado oil and season them with ½ teaspoon of the salt.

2   Place the mushrooms in the Salter air fryer basket and cook for 7 to 8 minutes, until fork-tender and soft to the touch.

While the mushrooms cook, in a small bowl mix together the remaining ½ teaspoon of salt, the garlic powder, pepper, onion powder, and paprika. Sprinkle the hamburger patties with the seasoning mixture. When the mushrooms are done cooking, remove them from the air fryer and place them on a serving platter with the cap side down.

Place the hamburger patties in the air fryer and cook for 7 minutes, or until the internal temperature reaches 145°F for a medium-done burger. Place a slice of Swiss cheese on each patty and cook for another minute to melt the cheese. Place the burgers on top of the mushrooms and drizzle with condiments of your choice. Best served fresh.

Per serving: Calories 345; Fat 23g; Protein 30g; Total carbs 5g; Fiber 1g

Air Fryer Steak Tips

PREP: 5 MINUTES PLUS 1 HOUR TO MARINATE • COOK TIME: 8 MINUTES • TOTAL: 1 HOUR 13 MINUTES• SERVES: 4

Ingredients

⅓ cup soy sauce

1 cup water

¼ cup freshly squeezed lemon juice

3 tablespoons brown sugar

1 teaspoon garlic powder

1 teaspoon ground ginger

1 teaspoon dried parsley

2 pounds steak tips, cut into 1-inch cubes

Instructions:

1 In a large mixing bowl, make the marinade. Mix together the soy sauce, water, lemon juice, brown sugar, garlic powder, ginger, and parsley. Place the meat in the marinade, then cover and refrigerate for at least 1 hour. Preheat the Salter air fryer to 400°F. Spray the Salter air fryer basket with olive oil. When the steak is done marinating, place it in the greased air fryer basket.

2 Set the timer and cook for 4 minutes. Using tongs, flip the meat. Reset the timer and cook for 4 minutes more.

Per Serving: Calories: 347; Fat: 9g; Saturated fat: 1g; Carbohydrate: 9g; Fiber: 0g; Sugar: 7g; Protein: 53g; Iron: 1mg; Sodium: 1203mg

Creamy Burger & Potato Bake

PREP: 5 MINUTES • COOK TIME: 55 MINUTES • TOTAL: 60 MINUTES • SERVES: 3

Ingredients

salt to taste

freshly ground pepper, to taste

1/2 (10.75 ounce) can condensed cream of mushroom soup

1/2-pound lean ground beef

1-1/2 cups peeled and thinly sliced potatoes

1/2 cup shredded Cheddar cheese

1/4 cup chopped onion

1/4 cup and 2 tablespoons milk

Instructions:

1 Lightly grease baking pan of air fryer with cooking spray. Add ground beef. For 10 minutes, cook on 360°F. Stir and crumble halfway through cooking time. Meanwhile, in a bowl, whisk well pepper, salt, milk, onion, and mushroom soup. Mix well. Drain fat off ground beef and transfer beef to a plate. In same air fryer baking pan, layer ½ of potatoes on bottom, then ½ of soup mixture, and then ½ of beef. Repeat process. Cover pan with foil.

2 Cook for 30 minutes. Remove foil and cook for another 15 minutes or until potatoes are tender. Serve and enjoy.

Per Serving: Calories: 399; Fat: 26.9g; Protein:22.1g

Beef Stroganoff

PREP: 10 MINUTES • COOK TIME: 14 MINUTES • TOTAL: 24 MINUTES • SERVES: 4

Ingredients

9 Ozs Tender Beef

1 Onion, chopped

1 Tbsp Paprika

3/4 Cup Sour Cream

Salt and Pepper to taste

Baking Dish

Instructions:

1. Preheat the Salter air fryer to 390 degrees.

2. Chop the beef and marinate it with the paprika. Add the chopped onions into the baking dish and heat for about 2 minutes in the Air fryer. When the onions are transparent, add the beef into the dish and cook for 5 minutes. Once the beef is starting to tender, pour in the sour cream and cook for another 7 minutes. At this point, the liquid should have reduced. Season with salt and pepper and serve.

Seafood Recipes

Coconut Shrimp
PREP: 5 MINUTES • COOK TIME: 10 MINUTES • TOTAL: 15 MINUTES • SERVES: 3

Ingredients

1 C. almond flour
1 C. panko breadcrumbs
1 tbsp. coconut flour

1 C. unsweetened, dried coconut
1 egg white
12 raw large shrimp

Instructions:

1   Put shrimp on paper towels to drain.
    Mix coconut and panko breadcrumbs together. Then mix in coconut flour and almond flour in a different bowl. Set to the side. Dip shrimp into flour mixture, then into egg white, and then into coconut mixture. Place into air fryer basket. Repeat with remaining shrimp.
2   Set temperature to 350°F, and set time to 10 minutes. Turn halfway through cooking process.

Per Serving: Calories:213; Fat: 8g; Protein:15g; Sugar:3g

Air Fryer Cajun Shrimp
PREP: 5 MINUTES • COOK TIME: 6 MINUTES • TOTAL: 11 MINUTES • SERVES: 2

Ingredients

12 ounces uncooked medium shrimp, peeled and deveined
1 teaspoon cayenne pepper
1 teaspoon Old Bay seasoning

½ teaspoon smoked paprika
2 tablespoons olive oil
1 teaspoon salt

Instructions:

1   Preheat the Salter air fryer to 390°F.
    Meanwhile, in a medium mixing bowl, combine the shrimp, cayenne pepper, Old Bay, paprika, olive oil, and salt. Toss the shrimp in the oil and spices until the shrimp is thoroughly coated with both.
2   Place the shrimp in the air fryer basket. Set the timer and steam for 3 minutes. Remove the drawer and shake, so the shrimp redistribute in the basket for even cooking. Reset the timer and steam for another 3 minutes. Check that the shrimp are done. When they are cooked through, the flesh will be opaque. Add additional time if needed. Plate, serve, and enjoy!

Per Serving: Calories: 286; Fat: 16g; Saturated fat: 2g; Carbohydrate: 1g; Fiber: 0g; Sugar: 0g; Protein: 37g; Iron: 6mg; Sodium: 1868mg

Grilled Salmon
PREP: 5 MINUTES • COOK TIME: 10 MINUTES • TOTAL: 15 MINUTES • SERVES: 3

Ingredients

2 Salmon Fillets
1/2 Tsp Lemon Pepper
1/2 Tsp Garlic Powder
Salt and Pepper

1/3 Cup Soy Sauce
1/3 Cup Sugar
1 Tbsp Olive Oil

Instructions:

1   Season salmon fillets with lemon pepper, garlic powder and salt. In a shallow bowl, add a third cup of water and combine the olive oil, soy sauce and sugar. Place salmon the bowl and immerse in the sauce. Cover with cling film and allow to marinate in the refrigerator for at least an hour
2   Preheat the Salter air fryer at 350 degrees.
    Place salmon into the Air fryer and cook for 10 minutes or more until the fish is tender. Serve with lemon wedges

Homemade Air Fried Crab Cake Sliders
PREP: 5 MINUTES • COOK TIME: 10 MINUTES • TOTAL: 15 MINUTES • SERVES: 4

Ingredients

1 pound crabmeat, shredded
¼ cup bread crumbs
2 teaspoons dried parsley
1 teaspoon salt
½ teaspoon freshly ground black pepper
1 large egg

2 tablespoons mayonnaise
1 teaspoon dry mustard
4 slider buns
Sliced tomato, lettuce leaves, and rémoulade sauce, for topping

Instructions:

1. Spray the Salter air fryer basket with olive oil or spray an air fryer–size baking sheet with olive oil or cooking spray.
   In a medium mixing bowl, combine the crabmeat, bread crumbs, parsley, salt, pepper, egg, mayonnaise, and dry mustard. Mix well.
   Form the crab mixture into 4 equal patties. (If the patties are too wet, add an additional 1 to 2 tablespoons of bread crumbs.)
   Place the crab cakes directly into the greased air fryer basket, or on the greased baking sheet set into the air fryer basket.
2. Set the temperature of your Salter AF to 400°F. Set the timer and fry for 5 minutes.
   Flip the crab cakes. Reset the timer and fry the crab cakes for 5 minutes more.
   Serve on slider buns with sliced tomato, lettuce, and rémoulade sauce.

Per Serving: Calories: 294; Fat: 11g; Saturated fat: 2g; Carbohydrate: 20g; Fiber: 1g; Sugar: 3g; Protein: 27g; Iron: 2mg; Sodium: 1766mg

Air Fried Lobster Tails
PREP: 5 MINUTES • COOK TIME: 8 MINUTES • TOTAL: 13 MINUTES • SERVES: 2

Ingredients

2 tablespoons unsalted butter, melted
1 tablespoon minced garlic
1 teaspoon salt

1 tablespoon minced fresh chives
2 (4- to 6-ounce) frozen lobster tails

Instructions:

1. In a small mixing bowl, combine the butter, garlic, salt, and chives.
   Butterfly the lobster tail: Starting at the meaty end of the tail, use kitchen shears to cut down the center of the top shell. Stop when you reach the fanned, wide part of the tail. Carefully spread apart the meat and the shell along the cut line, but keep the meat attached where it connects to the wide part of the tail. Use your hand to gently disconnect the meat from the bottom of the shell. Lift the meat up and out of the shell (keeping it attached at the wide end). Close the shell under the meat, so the meat rests on top of the shell.
   Place the lobster in the Salter air fryer basket and generously brush the butter mixture over the meat.
2. Set the temperature of your Salter AF to 380°F. Set the timer and steam for 4 minutes.
   Open the air fryer and rotate the lobster tails. Brush them with more of the butter mixture. Reset the timer and steam for 4 minutes more. The lobster is done when the meat is opaque.

Per Serving: Calories: 255; Fat: 13g; Saturated fat: 7g; Carbohydrate: 2g; Fiber: 0g; Sugar: 0g; Protein: 32g; Iron: 0mg; Sodium: 1453mg

Crispy Paprika Fish Fillets
PREP: 5 MINUTES • COOK TIME: 15 MINUTES • TOTAL: 20 MINUTES • SERVES: 4

Ingredients
1/2 cup seasoned breadcrumbs
1 tablespoon balsamic vinegar
1/2 teaspoon seasoned salt
1 teaspoon paprika

1/2 teaspoon ground black pepper
1 teaspoon celery seed
2 fish fillets, halved
1 egg, beaten

Instructions:
1   Add the breadcrumbs, vinegar, salt, paprika, ground black pepper, and celery seeds to your food processor. Process for about 30 seconds.
    Coat the fish fillets with the beaten egg; then, coat them with the breadcrumbs mixture.
2   Cook at 350 degrees F for about 15 minutes.

Bacon Wrapped Shrimp
PREP: 5 MINUTES • COOK TIME: 5 MINUTES • TOTAL: 10 MINUTES • SERVES: 4

Ingredients
1¼ pound tiger shrimp, peeled and deveined
1 pound bacon

Instructions:
1   Wrap each shrimp with a slice of bacon.
    Refrigerate for about 20 minutes. Preheat the Salter air fryer to 390 degrees F.
2   Arrange the shrimp in the Air fryer basket. Cook for about 5-7 minutes.

Bacon-Wrapped Scallops
PREP: 5 MINUTES • COOK TIME: 10 MINUTES • TOTAL: 15 MINUTES • SERVES: 4

Ingredients
16 sea scallops
8 slices bacon, cut in half
8 toothpicks

Salt
Freshly ground black pepper

Instructions:
1   Using a paper towel, pat dry the scallops.
    Wrap each scallop with a half slice of bacon. Secure the bacon with a toothpick.
    Place the scallops into the air fryer in a single layer. (You may need to cook your scallops in more than one batch.)
    Spray the scallops with olive oil, and season them with salt and pepper.
2   Set the temperature of your Salter AF to 370°F. Set the timer and fry for 5 minutes.
    Flip the scallops.
    Reset your timer and cook the scallops for 5 minutes more.
    Using tongs, remove the scallops from the air fryer basket. Plate, serve, and enjoy!

Per Serving: Calories: 311; Fat: 17g; Saturated fat: 5g; Carbohydrate: 3g; Fiber: 0g; Sugar: 0g; Protein: 34g; Iron: 1mg; Sodium: 1110mg

Air Fryer Salmon

PREP: 5 MINUTES • COOK TIME: 10 MINUTES • TOTAL: 15 MINUTES • SERVES: 2

Ingredients

½ tsp. salt
½ tsp. garlic powder

½ tsp. smoked paprika
Salmon

Instructions:

1. Mix spices together and sprinkle onto salmon. Place seasoned salmon into the Air fryer.
2. Close crisping lid. Set temperature to 400°F, and set time to 10 minutes.

Per Serving: Calories: 185; Fat: 11g; Protein:21g; Sugar:0g

Lemon Pepper, Butter, And Cajun Cod

PREP: 5 MINUTES • COOK TIME: 12 MINUTES • TOTAL: 17 MINUTES • SERVES: 2

Ingredients

2 (8-ounce) cod fillets, cut to fit into the air fryer basket
1 tablespoon Cajun seasoning
½ teaspoon lemon pepper

1 teaspoon salt
½ teaspoon freshly ground black pepper
2 tablespoons unsalted butter, melted
1 lemon, cut into 4 wedges

Instructions:

1. Spray the Salter air fryer basket with olive oil. Place the fillets on a plate. In a small mixing bowl, combine the Cajun seasoning, lemon pepper, salt, and pepper.
   Rub the seasoning mix onto the fish.
   Place the cod into the greased air fryer basket. Brush the top of each fillet with melted butter.
2. Set the temperature of your Salter AF to 360°F. Set the timer and bake for 6 minutes. After 6 minutes, open up your air fryer drawer and flip the fish. Brush the top of each fillet with more melted butter.
   Reset the timer and bake for 6 minutes more. Squeeze fresh lemon juice over the fillets.

Per Serving: Calories: 283; Fat: 14g; Saturated fat: 7g; Carbohydrate: 0g; Fiber: 0g; Sugar: 0g; Protein: 40g; Iron: 0mg; Sodium: 1460mg

Steamed Salmon & Sauce

PREP: 5 MINUTES • COOK TIME: 10 MINUTES • TOTAL: 15 MINUTES • SERVES: 2

Ingredients

1 cup Water
2 x 6 oz Fresh Salmon
2 Tsp Vegetable Oil
A Pinch of Salt for Each Fish
½ cup Plain Greek Yogurt

½ cup Sour Cream
2 Tbsp Finely Chopped Dill (Keep a bit for garnishing)
A Pinch of Salt to Taste

Instructions:

1. Pour the water into the bottom of the fryer and start heating to 285° F.
   Drizzle oil over the fish and spread it. Salt the fish to taste.
2. Now pop it into the fryer for 10 min.
   In the meantime, mix the yogurt, cream, dill and a bit of salt to make the sauce. When the fish is done, serve with the sauce and garnish with sprigs of dill.

Salmon Patties

PREP: 5 MINUTES • COOK TIME: 10 MINUTES • TOTAL: 15 MINUTES • SERVES: 4

Ingredients

1 (14.75-ounce) can wild salmon, drained
1 large egg
¼ cup diced onion
½ cup bread crumbs

1 teaspoon dried dill
½ teaspoon freshly ground black pepper
1 teaspoon salt
1 teaspoon Old Bay seasoning

Instructions:

1   Spray the Salter air fryer basket with olive oil. Put the salmon in a medium bowl and remove any bones or skin. Add the egg, onion, bread crumbs, dill, pepper, salt, and Old Bay seasoning and mix well. Form the salmon mixture into 4 equal patties. Place the patties in the greased air fryer basket.

2   Set the temperature of your Salter AF to 370°F. Set the timer and grill for 5 minutes. Flip the patties. Reset the timer and grill the patties for 5 minutes more. Plate, serve, and enjoy.

Per Serving: Calories: 239; Fat: 9g; Saturated fat: 2g; Carbohydrate: 11g; Fiber: 1g; Sugar: 1g; Protein: 27g; Iron: 2mg; Sodium: 901mg

Sweet And Savory Breaded Shrimp

PREP: 5 MINUTES • COOK TIME: 20 MINUTES • TOTAL: 25 MINUTES • SERVES: 2

Ingredients

½ pound of fresh shrimp, peeled from their shells and rinsed
2 raw eggs
½ cup of breadcrumbs (we like Panko, but any brand or home recipe will do)
½ white onion, peeled and rinsed and finely chopped
1 teaspoon of ginger-garlic paste

½ teaspoon of turmeric powder
½ teaspoon of red chili powder
½ teaspoon of cumin powder
½ teaspoon of black pepper powder
½ teaspoon of dry mango powder
Pinch of salt

Instructions:

1   Cover the basket of the Air fryer with a lining of tin foil, leaving the edges uncovered to allow air to circulate through the basket.
Preheat the Salter air fryer to 350 degrees. In a large mixing bowl, beat the eggs until fluffy and until the yolks and whites are fully combined. Dunk all the shrimp in the egg mixture, fully submerging. In a separate mixing bowl, combine the bread crumbs with all the dry ingredients until evenly blended. One by one, coat the egg-covered shrimp in the mixed dry ingredients so that fully covered, and place on the foil-lined air-fryer basket.

2   Set the air-fryer timer to 20 minutes. Halfway through the cooking time, shake the handle of the air-fryer so that the breaded shrimp jostles inside and fry-coverage is even. After 20 minutes, when the fryer shuts off, the shrimp will be perfectly cooked and their breaded crust golden-brown and delicious! Using tongs, remove from the air fryer and set on a serving dish to cool.

Healthy Fish and Chips
PREP: 5 MINUTES • COOK TIME: 15 MINUTES • TOTAL: 20 MINUTES • SERVES: 3

Ingredients
Old Bay seasoning
½ C. panko breadcrumbs
1 egg

2 tbsp. almond flour
4-6 ounce tilapia fillets
Frozen crinkle cut fries

Instructions:
1 Add almond flour to one bowl, beat egg in another bowl, and add panko breadcrumbs to the third bowl, mixed with Old Bay seasoning. Dredge tilapia in flour, then egg, and then breadcrumbs. Place coated fish in Air fryer along with fries.
2 Set temperature to 390°F, and set time to 15 minutes.

Per Serving: Calories: 219; Fat: 5g; Protein:25g; Sugar:1g

Indian Fish Fingers
PREP: 35 MINUTES • COOK TIME: 15 MINUTES • TOTAL: 50 MINUTES • SERVES: 4

Ingredients
1/2 pound fish fillet
1 tablespoon finely chopped fresh mint leaves or any fresh herbs
1/3 cup bread crumbs
1 teaspoon ginger garlic paste or ginger and garlic powders
1 hot green chili finely chopped

1/2 teaspoon paprika
Generous pinch of black pepper
Salt to taste
3/4 tablespoons lemon juice
3/4 teaspoons garam masala powder
1/3 teaspoon rosemary
1 egg

Instructions:
1 Start by removing any skin on the fish, washing, and patting dry. Cut the fish into fingers. In a medium bowl mix together all ingredients except for fish, mint, and bread crumbs. Bury the fingers in the mixture and refrigerate for 30 minutes. Remove from the bowl from the fridge and mix in mint leaves. In a separate bowl beat the egg, pour bread crumbs into a third bowl. Dip the fingers in the egg bowl then toss them in the bread crumbs bowl.
2 Cook at 360 degrees for 15 minutes, toss the fingers halfway through.

Per Serving: Calories: 187; Fat: 7g; Protein:11g; Fiber:1g

Lemon, Garlic, And Herb Salmon
PREP: 5 MINUTES • COOK TIME: 10 MINUTES • TOTAL: 15 MINUTES • SERVES: 4

Ingredients
3 tablespoons unsalted butter
1 garlic clove, minced, or ½ teaspoon garlic powder
1 teaspoon salt
2 tablespoons freshly squeezed lemon juice
1 tablespoon minced fresh parsley

1 teaspoon minced fresh dill
1 teaspoon salt
½ teaspoon freshly ground black pepper
4 (4-ounce) salmon fillets

Instructions:
1 Line the Salter air fryer basket with parchment paper.
   In a small microwave-safe mixing bowl, combine the butter, garlic, salt, lemon juice, parsley, dill, salt, and pepper. Place the bowl in the microwave and cook on low until the butter is completely melted, about 45 seconds. Meanwhile, place the salmon fillets in the parchment-lined air fryer basket. Spoon the sauce over the salmon.
2 Set the temperature of your Salter AF to 400°F. Set the timer and bake for 10 minutes. Since you don't want to overcook the salmon, begin checking for doneness at about 8 minutes. Salmon is done when the flesh is opaque and flakes easily when tested with a fork.

Shrimp Scampi
PREP: 5 MINUTES • COOK TIME: 8 MINUTES • TOTAL: 13 MINUTES • SERVES: 4

Ingredients

¼ cup unsalted butter (or butter-flavored coconut oil for dairy-free)

2 tablespoons fish stock or chicken broth

1 tablespoon lemon juice

2 cloves garlic, minced

2 tablespoons chopped fresh basil leaves

1 tablespoon chopped fresh parsley, plus more for garnish

1 teaspoon red pepper flakes

1 pound large shrimp, peeled and deveined, tails removed

Fresh basil sprigs, for garnish

Instructions:

1. Preheat the Salter air fryer to 350° F. Place the butter, fish stock, lemon juice, garlic, basil, parsley, and red pepper flakes in a 6 by 3-inch pan, stir to combine, and place in the air fryer.
2. Cook for 3 minutes, or until fragrant and the garlic has softened.
   Add the shrimp and stir to coat the shrimp in the sauce. Cook for 5 minutes, or until the shrimp are pink, stirring after 3 minutes. Garnish with fresh basil sprigs and chopped parsley before serving. Store leftovers in an airtight container in the refrigerator for up to 4 days. Reheat in a preheated 400°F air fryer for about 3 minutes, until heated through.

Per serving: Calories 175; Fat 11g; Protein 18g; Total carbs 1g; Fiber 0.2g

Simple Scallops
PREP: 5 MINUTES • COOK TIME: 4 MINUTES • TOTAL: 9 MINUTES • SERVES: 2

Ingredients

12 medium sea scallops

1 teaspoon fine sea salt

¾ teaspoon ground black pepper, plus more for garnish if desired

Fresh thyme leaves, for garnish (optional)

Instructions:

1. Spray the Salter air fryer basket with avocado oil. Preheat the Salter air fryer to 390°F. Rinse the scallops and pat completely dry. Spray avocado oil on the scallops and season them with the salt and pepper.
2. Place them in the air fryer basket, spacing them apart (if you're using a smaller air fryer, work in batches if necessary). Cook for 2 minutes, then flip the scallops and cook for another 2 minutes, or until cooked through and no longer translucent. Garnish with ground black pepper and thyme leaves, if desired. Best served fresh. Store leftovers in an airtight container in the fridge for up to 3 days. Reheat in a preheated 350°F air fryer for 2 minutes, or until heated through.

Quick Paella
PREP: 7 MINUTES • COOK TIME: 15 MINUTES • TOTAL: 22 MINUTES • SERVES: 4

Ingredients

1 (10-ounce) package frozen cooked rice, thawed

1 (6-ounce) jar artichoke hearts, drained and chopped

¼ cup vegetable broth

½ teaspoon turmeric

½ teaspoon dried thyme

1 cup frozen cooked small shrimp

½ cup frozen baby peas

1 tomato, diced

Instructions:

1. In a 6-by-6-by-2-inch pan, combine the rice, artichoke hearts, vegetable broth, turmeric, and thyme, and stir gently.
2. Place in the Air fryer and bake for 8 to 9 minutes or until the rice is hot. Remove from the air fryer and gently stir in the shrimp, peas, and tomato. Cook for 5 to 8 minutes or until the shrimp and peas are hot and the paella is bubbling.

Tuna Melt Croquettes

PREP: 5 MINUTES • COOK TIME: 10 MINUTES • TOTAL: 15 MINUTES • SERVES: 1 Dozen Croquettes

Ingredients

2 (5-ounce) cans tuna, drained
1 (8-ounce) package cream cheese, softened
½ cup finely shredded cheddar cheese
2 tablespoons diced onions
2 teaspoons prepared yellow mustard
1 large egg

1½ cups pork dust or powdered Parmesan cheese
Fresh dill, for garnish (optional)
FOR SERVING (OPTIONAL):
Cherry tomatoes
Mayonnaise
Prepared yellow mustard

Instructions:

1 Preheat the Salter air fryer to 400°F.
   Make the patties: In a large bowl, stir together the tuna, cream cheese, cheddar cheese, onions, mustard, and egg until well combined. Place the pork dust in a shallow bowl.
   Form the tuna mixture into twelve 1½-inch balls. Roll the balls in the pork dust and use your hands to press it into a thick crust around each ball. Flatten the balls into ½-inch-thick patties.

2 Working in batches to avoid overcrowding, place the patties in the air fryer basket, leaving space between them. Cook for 8 minutes, or until golden brown and crispy, flipping halfway through. Garnish the croquettes with fresh dill, if desired, and serve with cherry tomatoes and dollops of mayo and mustard on the side.
   Store leftovers in an airtight container in the refrigerator for up to 4 days. Reheat in a preheated 400°F air fryer for about 3 minutes, until heated through.

Per serving: Calories 528; Fat 36g; Protein 48g; Total carbs 2g; Fiber 0.3g

Coconut Shrimp

PREP: 15 MINUTES • COOK TIME: 5 MINUTES • TOTAL: 20 MINUTES • SERVES: 4

Ingredients

1 (8-ounce) can crushed pineapple
½ cup sour cream
¼ cup pineapple preserves
2 egg whites
⅔ cup cornstarch

⅔ cup sweetened coconut
1 cup panko bread crumbs
1 pound uncooked large shrimp, thawed if frozen, deveined and shelled
Olive oil for misting

Instructions:

1 Drain the crushed pineapple well, reserving the juice. In a small bowl, combine the pineapple, sour cream, and preserves, and mix well. Set aside. In a shallow bowl, beat the egg whites with 2 tablespoons of the reserved pineapple liquid. Place the cornstarch on a plate. Combine the coconut and bread crumbs on another plate. Dip the shrimp into the cornstarch, shake it off, then dip into the egg white mixture and finally into the coconut mixture. Place the shrimp in the Salter air fryer basket and mist with oil.

2 Air-fry for 5 to 7 minutes or until the shrimp are crisp and golden brown.

Per Serving: Calories: 524; Fat: 14g; Protein:33g; Fiber:4g

Sweet Recipes

Perfect Cinnamon Toast
PREP: 10 MINUTES • COOK TIME: 5 MINUTES • TOTAL: 15 MINUTES •*SERVES: 6*

Ingredients

2 tsp. pepper

1 ½ tsp. vanilla extract

1 ½ tsp. cinnamon

½ C. sweetener of choice

1 C. coconut oil

12 slices whole wheat bread

Instructions:

1   Melt coconut oil and mix with sweetener until dissolved. Mix in remaining ingredients minus bread till incorporated. Spread mixture onto bread, covering all area.

2   Place coated pieces of bread in your Air fryer.
Cook 5 minutes at 400 degrees. Remove and cut diagonally. Enjoy.

Per Serving: Calories: 124; Fat:2g; Protein:0g; Sugar:4g

Easy Baked Chocolate Mug Cake
PREP: 5 MINUTES • COOK TIME: 15 MINUTES • TOTAL: 20 MINUTES • *SERVES: 3*

Ingredients

½ cup cocoa powder

½ cup stevia powder

1 cup coconut cream

1 package cream cheese, room temperature

1 tablespoon vanilla extract

4 tablespoons butter

Instructions:

1   Preheat the Salter air fryer for 5 minutes. In a mixing bowl, combine all ingredients. Use a hand mixer to mix everything until fluffy. Pour into greased mugs. Place the mugs in the fryer basket.

2   Bake for 15 minutes at 350°F.Place in the fridge to chill before serving.

Per Serving: Calories: 744; Fat:69.7g; Protein:13.9g; Sugar:4g

Easy Chocolate-Frosted Doughnuts
PREP: 5 MINUTES • COOK TIME: 5 MINUTES • TOTAL: 10 MINUTES • *SERVES: 6*

Ingredients

1 (16.3-ounce / 8-count) package refrigerated biscuit dough

¾ cup powdered sugar

¼ cup unsweetened cocoa powder

¼ cup milk

Instructions:

1   Spray the Salter air fryer basket with olive oil.
Unroll the biscuit dough onto a cutting board and separate the biscuits.
Using a 1-inch biscuit cutter or cookie cutter, cut out the center of each biscuit.
Place the doughnuts into the air fryer. (You may have to cook your doughnuts in more than one batch.)

2   Set the temperature of your Salter AF to 330°F. Set the timer and bake for 5 minutes.
Using tongs, remove the doughnuts from the air fryer and let them cool slightly before glazing.
Meanwhile, in a small mixing bowl, combine the powdered sugar, unsweetened cocoa powder, and milk and mix until smooth.
Dip your doughnuts into the glaze and use a knife to smooth the frosting evenly over the doughnut.
Let the glaze set before serving.

Per Serving (1 doughnut): Calories: 233; Fat: 8g; Saturated fat: 3g; Carbohydrate: 37g; Fiber: 2g; Sugar: 15g; Protein: 5g; Iron: 2mg; Sodium: 590mg

Air Fryer Homemade Pumpkin Fritters

PREP: 5 MINUTES • COOK TIME: 9 MINUTES • TOTAL: 14 MINUTES • *SERVES: 8 FRITTERS*

Ingredients

FOR THE FRITTERS

1 (16.3-ounce, 8-count) package refrigerated biscuit dough

½ cup chopped pecans

¼ cup pumpkin purée

¼ cup sugar

1 teaspoon pumpkin pie spice

2 tablespoons unsalted butter, melted

FOR THE GLAZE

1 cup powdered sugar

1 teaspoon pumpkin pie spice

1 tablespoon pumpkin purée

2 tablespoons milk (plus more to thin the glaze, if necessary)

Instructions:

1 TO MAKE THE FRITTERS. Spray the Salter air fryer basket with olive oil or spray an air fryer–size baking sheet with olive oil or cooking spray. Turn the biscuit dough out onto a cutting board. Cut each biscuit into 8 pieces. Once you cut all the pieces, place them in a medium mixing bowl. Add the pecans, pumpkin, sugar, and pumpkin pie spice to the biscuit pieces and toss until well combined. Shape the dough into 8 even mounds. Drizzle butter over each of the fritters.

2 Place the fritters directly in the greased air fryer basket, or on the greased baking sheet set in the air fryer basket. Set the temperature of your Salter AF to 330°F. Set the timer and bake for 7 minutes.

Check to see if the fritters are done. The dough should be cooked through and solid to the touch. If not, cook for 1 to 2 minutes more. Using tongs, gently remove the fritters from the air fryer. Let cool for about 10 minutes before you apply the glaze.

TO MAKE THE GLAZE

In a small mixing bowl, mix together the powdered sugar, pumpkin pie spice, pumpkin, and milk until smooth. If it seems more like icing, it is too thick. It should coat a spoon and be of a pourable consistency. Drizzle the glaze over the fritters.

Per Serving (1 fritter): Calories: 341; Fat: 16g; Saturated fat: 5g; Carbohydrate: 47g; Fiber: 2g; Sugar: 26g; Protein: 5g; Iron: 2mg; Sodium: 608mg

Angel Food Cake

PREP: 5 MINUTES • COOK TIME: 30 MINUTES • TOTAL: 35 MINUTES • *SERVES: 12*

Ingredients

¼ cup butter, melted

1 cup powdered erythritol

1 teaspoon strawberry extract

12 egg whites

2 teaspoons cream of tartar

A pinch of salt

Instructions:

1 Preheat the Salter air fryer for 5 minutes.

Mix the egg whites and cream of tartar. Use a hand mixer and whisk until white and fluffy.

Add the rest of the ingredients except for the butter and whisk for another minute.

Pour into a baking dish.

2 Place in the Salter air fryer basket and cook for 30 minutes at 400°F or if a toothpick inserted in the middle comes out clean. Drizzle with melted butter once cooled.

Per Serving: Calories: 65; Fat:5g; Protein:3.1g; Fiber:1g

Air Fryer Homemade Chocolate Chip Cookies
PREP: 5 MINUTES • COOK TIME: 5 MINUTES • TOTAL: 10 MINUTES • *SERVES: 25 COOKIES*

Ingredients

1 cup (2 sticks) unsalted butter, at room temperature
1 cup granulated sugar
1 cup brown sugar
2 large eggs
½ teaspoon vanilla extract

1 teaspoon baking soda
½ teaspoon salt
3 cups all-purpose flour
2 cups chocolate chips

Instructions:

1   Spray an air fryer–size baking sheet with cooking spray
    In a large bowl, cream the butter and both sugars. Mix in the eggs, vanilla, baking soda, salt, and flour until well combined. Fold in the chocolate chips. Use your hands and knead the dough together, so everything is well mixed. Using a cookie scoop or a tablespoon, drop heaping spoonfuls of dough onto the baking sheet about 1 inch apart Set the baking sheet into the air fryer. Set the temperature of your Salter AF to 340°F. Set the timer and bake for 5 minutes. When the cookies are golden brown and cooked through, use silicone oven mitts to remove the baking sheet from the air fryer and serve. If you line your Salter air fryer basket with air fryer parchment paper sprayed with cooking spray, you can cook multiple batches of cookies with very little cleanup.

Fried Peaches
PREP: 2 HOURS 10 MINUTES • COOK TIME: 15 MINUTES • TOTAL: 15 MINUTES • *SERVES: 4*

Ingredients

4 ripe peaches (1/2 a peach = 1 serving)
1 1/2 cups flour
Salt
2 egg yolks
3/4 cups cold water

1 1/2 tablespoons olive oil
2 tablespoons brandy
4 egg whites
Cinnamon/sugar mix

Instructions:

1   Mix flour, egg yolks, and salt in a mixing bowl. Slowly mix in water, then add brandy. Set the mixture aside for 2 hours and go do something for 1 hour 45 minutes.
    Boil a large pot of water and cut and X at the bottom of each peach. While the water boils fill another large bowl with water and ice. Boil each peach for about a minute, then plunge it in the ice bath. Now the peels should basically fall off the peach. Beat the egg whites and mix into the batter mix. Dip each peach in the mix to coat.
2   Cook at 360 degrees for 10 Minutes.
    Prepare a plate with cinnamon/sugar mix, roll peaches in mix and serve.

Per Serving: Calories: 306; Fat:3g; Protein:10g; Fiber:2.7g

Apple Dumplings
PREP: 10 MINUTES • COOK TIME: 25 MINUTES • TOTAL: 35 MINUTES • *SERVES: 4*

Ingredients

2 tbsp. melted coconut oil
2 puff pastry sheets
1 tbsp. brown sugar

2 tbsp. raisins
2 small apples of choice

Instructions:

1   Ensure your air fryer is preheated to 356 degrees.
    Core and peel apples and mix with raisins and sugar.
    Place a bit of apple mixture into puff pastry sheets and brush sides with melted coconut oil.
2   Place into the Air fryer. Cook 25 minutes, turning halfway through. Will be golden when done.

Air Fryer Stuffed Baked Apples
PREP: 5 MINUTES • COOK TIME: 20 MINUTES • TOTAL: 15 MINUTES • *SERVES: 4*

Ingredients
4 to 6 tablespoons chopped walnuts

4 to 6 tablespoons raisins

4 tablespoons (½ stick) unsalted butter, melted

1 teaspoon ground cinnamon

½ teaspoon ground nutmeg

4 apples, cored but with the bottoms left intact

Vanilla ice cream, for topping

Maple syrup, for topping

Instructions:
1 In a small mixing bowl, make the filling. Mix together the walnuts, raisins, melted butter, cinnamon, and nutmeg. Scoop a quarter of the filling into each apple. Place the apples in an air fryer–safe pan and set the pan in the air fryer basket.

2 Set the temperature of your Salter AF to 350°F. Set the timer and bake for 20 minutes.
Serve with vanilla ice cream and a drizzle of maple syrup. Variation Tip: If you'd like to make baked apples with oatmeal filling, just add 1 cup of rolled oats and ¼ cup of brown sugar to the filling.

Per Serving: Calories: 382; Fat: 19g; Saturated fat: 9g; Carbohydrate: 57g; Fiber: 7g; Sugar: 44g; Protein: 4g; Iron: 2mg; Sodium: 100mg

Easy Air Fried Apple Hand Pies
PREP: 5 MINUTES • COOK TIME: 7 MINUTES • TOTAL: 12 MINUTES • *SERVES: 8 HAND PIES*

Ingredients
1 package prepared pie dough

½ cup apple pie filling

1 large egg white

1 tablespoon Wilton White Sparkling Sugar

Caramel sauce, for drizzling

Instructions:
1 Spray the Salter air fryer basket with olive oil. Lightly flour a clean work surface. Lay out the dough on the work surface. Using a 2-inch biscuit cutter, cut out 8 circles from the dough. Gather up the scraps of dough, form them into a ball, and reroll them. Using the biscuit cutter, cut out the remaining dough. Add about 1 tablespoon of apple pie filling to the center of each circle. Fold over the dough and use a fork to seal the edges. Brush the egg white over the top, then sprinkle with sparkling sugar. Place the hand pies in the greased air fryer basket. They should be spaced so that they do not touch one another.

2 Set the temperature of your Salter AF to 350°F. Set the timer and bake for 5 minutes. When they are done, the crust should be golden brown. If they are not done, bake for another 2 minutes. Drizzle with caramel sauce, if desired.

Per Serving (1 pie): Calories: 120; Fat: 5g; Saturated fat: 1g; Carbohydrate: 17g; Fiber: 0g; Sugar: 3g; Protein: 1g; Iron: 0mg; Sodium: 144mg

Apple Pie in Air Fryer

PREP: 5 MINUTES • COOK TIME: 35 MINUTES • TOTAL: 40 MINUTES • *SERVES: 4*

Ingredients

½ teaspoon vanilla extract

1 beaten egg

1 large apple, chopped

1 Pillsbury Refrigerator pie crust

1 tablespoon butter

1 tablespoon ground cinnamon

1 tablespoon raw sugar

2 tablespoon sugar

2 teaspoons lemon juice

Baking spray

Instructions:

1   Lightly grease baking pan of air fryer with cooking spray. Spread pie crust on bottom of pan up to the sides. In a bowl, mix vanilla, sugar, cinnamon, lemon juice, and apples. Pour on top of pie crust. Top apples with butter slices. Cover apples with the other pie crust. Pierce with knife the tops of pie. Spread beaten egg on top of crust and sprinkle sugar. Cover with foil.

2   For 25 minutes, cook on 390°F. Remove foil cook for 10 minutes at 330oF until tops are browned. Serve and enjoy.

Easy Air Fryer Blueberry Pie

PREP: 5 MINUTES PLUS 30 MINUTES TO THAW • COOK TIME: 18 MINUTES • TOTAL: 53 MINUTES •*SERVES: 4-6*

Ingredients

2 frozen pie crusts

2 (21-ounce) jars blueberry pie filling

1 teaspoon milk

1 teaspoon sugar

Instructions:

1   Remove the pie crusts from the freezer and let them thaw for 30 minutes on the countertop. Place one crust into the bottom of a 6-inch pie pan. Pour the pie filling into the bottom crust, then cover it with the other crust, being careful to press the bottom and top crusts together around the edge to form a seal. Trim off any excess pie dough. Cut venting holes in the top crust with a knife or a small decoratively shaped cookie cutter. Brush the top crust with milk, then sprinkle the sugar over it. Place the pie in the air fryer basket.

2   Set the temperature of your Salter AF to 310°F. Set the timer and bake for 15 minutes.
Check the pie after 15 minutes. If it needs additional time, reset the timer and bake for an additional 3 minutes. Using silicone oven mitts, remove the pie from the air fryer and let cool for 15 minutes before serving.

Air Fryer Chocolate Cake

PREP: 5 MINUTES • COOK TIME: 35 MINUTES • TOTAL: 40 MINUTES • *SERVES: 8-10*

Ingredients

½ C. hot water

1 tsp. vanilla

¼ C. olive oil

½ C. almond milk

1 egg

½ tsp. salt

¾ tsp. baking soda

¾ tsp. baking powder

½ C. unsweetened cocoa powder

2 C. almond flour

1 C. brown sugar

Instructions:

1   Preheat your air fryer to 356 degrees.
Stir all dry ingredients together. Then stir in wet ingredients. Add hot water last.
The batter will be thin, no worries.

2   Pour cake batter into a pan that fits into the fryer. Cover with foil and poke holes into the foil. Bake 35 minutes. Discard foil and then bake another 10 minutes.

Per Serving: Calories: 378; Fat:9g; Protein:4g; Sugar:5g

Raspberry Cream Rol-Ups

PREP: 10 MINUTES • COOK TIME: 25 MINUTES • TOTAL: 35 MINUTES • *SERVES: 4*

Ingredients

1 cup of fresh raspberries, rinsed and patted dry
½ cup of cream cheese, softened to room temperature
¼ cup of brown sugar
¼ cup of sweetened condensed milk

1 egg
1 teaspoon of corn starch
6 spring roll wrappers
¼ cup of water

Instructions:

1   Cover the basket of the Air fryer with a lining of tin foil, leaving the edges uncovered to allow air to circulate through the basket. Preheat the Salter air fryer to 350 degrees. In a mixing bowl, combine the cream cheese, brown sugar, condensed milk, cornstarch, and egg. Beat or whip thoroughly, until all ingredients are completely mixed and fluffy, thick and stiff. Spoon even amounts of the creamy filling into each spring roll wrapper, then top each dollop of filling with several raspberries. Roll up the wraps around the creamy raspberry filling, and seal the seams with a few dabs of water. Place each roll on the foil-lined Air fryer basket, seams facing down.

2   Set the Salter air fryer timer to 10 minutes. During cooking, shake the handle of the fryer basket to ensure a nice even surface crisp. After 10 minutes, when the Air fryer shuts off, the spring rolls should be golden brown and perfect on the outside, while the raspberries and cream filling will have cooked together in a glorious fusion. Remove with tongs and serve hot or cold.

Air Fryer Banana Cake

PREP: 5 MINUTES • COOK TIME: 30 MINUTES • TOTAL: 35 MINUTES • *SERVES: 4*

Ingredients

⅓ cup brown sugar
4 tablespoons (½ stick) unsalted butter, at room temperature
1 ripe banana, mashed
1 large egg

2 tablespoons granulated sugar
1 cup all-purpose flour
1 teaspoon ground cinnamon
1 teaspoon vanilla extract
½ teaspoon ground nutmeg

Instructions:

1   Spray a 6-inch Bundt pan with cooking spray.
In a medium mixing bowl, cream the brown sugar and butter until pale and fluffy.
Mix in the banana and egg. Add the granulated sugar, flour, ground cinnamon, vanilla, and nutmeg and mix well. Spoon the batter into the prepared pan. Place the pan in the air fryer basket.

2   Set the temperature of your Salter AF to 320°F. Set the timer and bake for 15 minutes.
Do a toothpick test. If the toothpick comes out clean, the cake is done. It there is batter on the toothpick, cook and check again in 5-minute intervals until the cake is done. It will likely take about 30 minutes total baking time to fully cook. Using silicone oven mitts, remove the Bundt pan from the air fryer. Set the pan on a wire cooling rack and let cool for about 10 minutes. Place a plate upside-down (like a lid) over the top of the Bundt pan. Carefully flip the plate and the pan over, and set the plate on the counter. Lift the Bundt pan off the cake. Frost as desired.

Per Serving: Calories: 334; Fat: 13g; Saturated fat: 8g; Carbohydrate: 49g; Fiber: 2g; Sugar: 22g; Protein: 5g; Iron: 2mg; Sodium: 104mg

Banana-Choco Brownies

PREP: 5 MINUTES • COOK TIME: 30 MINUTES • TOTAL: 35 MINUTES • *SERVES: 12*

Ingredients

2 cups almond flour
2 teaspoons baking powder
½ teaspoon baking powder
½ teaspoon baking soda
½ teaspoon salt
1 over-ripe banana

3 large eggs
½ teaspoon stevia powder
¼ cup coconut oil
1 tablespoon vinegar
1/3 cup almond flour
1/3 cup cocoa powder

Instructions:

1   Preheat the Salter air fryer for 5 minutes. Combine all ingredients in a food processor and pulse until well-combined. Pour into a baking dish that will fit in the air fryer.

2   Place in the Salter air fryer basket and cook for 30 minutes at 350°F or if a toothpick inserted in the middle comes out clean.

Per Serving: Calories: 75; Fat:6.5g; Protein:1.7g; Sugar:2g

Easy Air Fried Old-Fashioned Cherry Cobbler

PREP: 5 MINUTES • COOK TIME: 35 MINUTES • TOTAL: 15 MINUTES • *SERVES: 4*

Ingredients

1 cup all-purpose flour
1 cup sugar
2 tablespoons baking powder

¾ cup milk
8 tablespoons (1 stick) unsalted butter
1 (21-ounce) can cherry pie filling

Instructions:

1   In a small mixing bowl, mix together the flour, sugar, and baking powder. Add the milk and mix until well blended. Melt the butter in a small microwave-safe bowl in the microwave, about 45 seconds. Pour the butter into the bottom of an 8-by-8-inch pan, then pour in the batter and spread it in an even layer. Pour the pie filing over the batter. Do not mix; the batter will bubble up through the filling durin cooking.

2   Set the temperature of your Salter AF to 320°F. Set the timer and bake for 20 minutes.
Check the cobbler. When the cobbler is done the batter will be golden brown and cooked through. If not done, bake and recheck for doneness in 5-minute intervals. Overall cooking time will likely be between 30 and 35 minutes. Remove from the air fryer and let cool slightly before serving.

Per Serving: Calories: 706; Fat: 24g; Saturated fat: 15g; Carbohydrate: 121g; Fiber: 2g; Sugar: 52g; Protein: 6g; Iron: 2mg; Sodium: 219mg

Chocolate Donuts

PREP: 5 MINUTES • COOK TIME: 20 MINUTES • TOTAL: 25 MINUTES • *SERVES: 8-10*

Ingredients

(8-ounce) can jumbo biscuits
Cooking oil

Chocolate sauce, such as Hershey's

Instructions:

1   Separate the biscuit dough into 8 biscuits and place them on a flat work surface. Use a small circle cookie cutter or a biscuit cutter to cut a hole in the center of each biscuit. You can also cut the holes using a knife.
Spray the Salter air fryer basket with cooking oil.

2   Place 4 donuts in the air fryer. Do not stack. Spray with cooking oil. Cook for 4 minutes.
Open the air fryer and flip the donuts. Cook for an additional 4 minutes.
Remove the cooked donuts from the air fryer, then repeat steps 3 and 4 for the remaining 4 donuts.
Drizzle chocolate sauce over the donuts and enjoy while warm.

Per Serving: Calories: 181; Fat:98g; Protein:3g; Fiber:1g

Homemade Air Fried Fudge Brownies
PREP: 5 MINUTES • COOK TIME: 20 MINUTES • TOTAL: 25 MINUTES • *SERVES: 6*

Ingredients

8 tablespoons (1 stick) unsalted butter, melted

1 cup sugar

1 teaspoon vanilla extract

2 large eggs

½ cup all-purpose flour

½ cup cocoa powder

1 teaspoon baking powder

Instructions:

1. Spray a 6-inch air fryer–safe baking pan with cooking spray or grease the pan with butter. In a medium mixing bowl, mix together the butter and sugar, then add the vanilla and eggs and beat until well combined. Add the flour, cocoa powder, and baking powder and mix until smooth. Pour the batter into the prepared pan.
2. Set the temperature of your Salter AF to 350°F. Set the timer and bake for 20 minutes. Once the center is set, use silicon oven mitts to remove the pan from the air fryer. Let cool slightly before serving.

Chocolate Bundt Cake
PREP: 5 MINUTES • COOK TIME: 30 MINUTES • TOTAL: 35 MINUTES • *SERVES: 4*

Ingredients

1¾ cups all-purpose flour

2 cups sugar

¾ cup unsweetened cocoa powder

1 teaspoon baking soda

1 teaspoon baking powder

½ cup vegetable oil

1 teaspoon salt

2 teaspoons vanilla extract

2 large eggs

1 cup milk

1 cup hot water

Instructions:

1. Spray a 6-inch Bundt pan with cooking spray.
   In a large mixing bowl, combine the flour, sugar, cocoa powder, baking soda, baking powder, oil, salt, vanilla, eggs, milk, and hot water. Pour the cake batter into the prepared pan and set the pan in the air fryer basket.
2. Set the temperature of your Salter AF to 330°F. Set the timer and bake for 20 minutes. Do a toothpick test. If the toothpick comes out clean, the cake is done. It there is batter on the toothpick, cook and check again in 5-minute intervals until the cake is done. It will likely take about 30 minutes total baking time to fully cook. Using silicone oven mitts, remove the Bundt pan from the air fryer. Set the pan on a wire cooling rack and let cool for about 10 minutes. Place a plate upside down over the top of the Bundt pan. Carefully flip the plate and the pan over, and set the plate on the counter. Lift the Bundt pan off the cake.

Per Serving: Calories: 924; Fat: 34g; Saturated fat: 6g; Carbohydrate: 155g; Fiber: 6g; Sugar: 104g; Protein: 14g; Iron: 6mg; Sodium: 965mg

Easy Air Fryer Donuts
PREP: 5 MINUTES • COOK TIME: 5 MINUTES • TOTAL: 10 MINUTES • *SERVES: 8*

Ingredients

Pinch of allspice

4 tbsp. dark brown sugar

½ - 1 tsp. cinnamon

1/3 C. granulated sweetener

3 tbsp. melted coconut oil

1 can of biscuits

Instructions:

1. Mix allspice, sugar, sweetener, and cinnamon together.
   Take out biscuits from can and with a circle cookie cutter, cut holes from centers and place into air fryer.
2. Cook 5 minutes at 350 degrees. As batches are cooked, use a brush to coat with melted coconut oil and dip each into sugar mixture.
   Serve warm.

Little French Fudge Cakes

PREP: 10 MINUTES • COOK TIME: 25 MINUTES • TOTAL: 35 MINUTES • *SERVES: 12 CAKES*

Ingredients

3 cups blanched almond flour

¾ cup unsweetened cocoa powder

1 teaspoon baking soda

½ teaspoon fine sea salt

6 large eggs

1 cup Swerve confectioners'-style sweetener

1½ cups canned pumpkin puree

3 tablespoons brewed decaf espresso or other strong brewed decaf coffee

3 tablespoons unsalted butter, melted but not hot

1 teaspoon vanilla extract

CREAM CHEESE FROSTING:

½ cup Swerve confectioners'-style sweetener

½ cup (1 stick) unsalted butter, melted

4 ounces cream cheese (½ cup) softened

3 tablespoons unsweetened, unflavored almond milk or heavy cream

CHOCOLATE DRIZZLE:

3 tablespoons unsalted butter

2 tablespoons Swerve confectioners'-style sweetener or liquid sweetener

2 tablespoons unsweetened cocoa powder

¼ cup unsweetened, unflavored almond milk

½ cup chopped walnuts or pecans, for garnish (optional)

Instructions:

1   Preheat the Salter air fryer to 350°F. Spray 2 mini Bundt pans with coconut oil.
In a medium-sized bowl, whisk together the flour, cocoa powder, baking soda, and salt until blended.
In a large bowl, beat the eggs and sweetener with a hand mixer for 2 to 3 minutes, until light and fluffy. Add the pumpkin puree, espresso, melted butter, and vanilla and stir to combine.
Add the wet ingredients to the dry ingredients and stir until just combined.
Pour the batter into the prepared pans, filling each well two-thirds full.

2   Cook in the air fryer for 20 to 25 minutes, until a toothpick inserted into the center of a cake comes out clean. Allow the cakes to cool completely in the pans before removing them. Make the frosting: In a large bowl, mix the sweetener, melted butter, and cream cheese until well combined. Add the almond milk and stir well to combine. Make the chocolate drizzle: In a small bowl, stir together the melted butter, sweetener, and cocoa powder until well combined. Add the almond milk while stirring to thin the mixture. After the cakes have cooled, dip the tops of the cakes into the frosting, then use a spoon to drizzle the chocolate over each frosted cake. If desired, garnish the cakes with chopped nuts.
Store leftovers in an airtight container in the refrigerator for up to 4 days or in the freezer for up to a month.

Chocolate Soufflé for Two

PREP: 5 MINUTES • COOK TIME: 14 MINUTES • TOTAL: 19 MINUTES • *SERVES: 2*

Ingredients

2 tbsp. almond flour

½ tsp. vanilla

3 tbsp. sweetener

2 separated eggs

¼ C. melted coconut oil

3 ounces of semi-sweet chocolate, chopped

Instructions:

1   Brush coconut oil and sweetener onto ramekins.
Melt coconut oil and chocolate together.
Beat egg yolks well, adding vanilla and sweetener. Stir in flour and ensure there are no lumps. Preheat fryer to 330 degrees. Whisk egg whites till they reach peak state and fold them into chocolate mixture. Pour batter into ramekins and place into the fryer.

2   Cook 14 minutes. Serve with powdered sugar dusted on top.

Per Serving: Calories: 238; Fat:6g; Protein:1g; Sugar:4g

Fried Bananas with Chocolate Sauce
PREP: 10 MINUTES • COOK TIME: 10 MINUTES • TOTAL: 20 MINUTES • *SERVES: 2*

Ingredients
1 large egg

¼ cup cornstarch

¼ cup plain bread crumbs

3 bananas, halved crosswise

Cooking oil

Chocolate sauce

Instructions:

1   In a small bowl, beat the egg. In another bowl, place the cornstarch. Place the bread crumbs in a third bowl. Dip the bananas in the cornstarch, then the egg, and then the bread crumbs.
Spray the Salter air fryer basket with cooking oil. Place the bananas in the basket and spray them with cooking oil.

2   Cook for 5 minutes. Open the air fryer and flip the bananas. Cook for an additional 2 minutes. Transfer the bananas to plates.
Drizzle the chocolate sauce over the bananas, and serve.
You can make your own chocolate sauce using 2 tablespoons milk and ¼ cup chocolate chips. Heat a saucepan over medium-high heat. Add the milk and stir for 1 to 2 minutes. Add the chocolate chips. Stir for 2 minutes, or until the chocolate has melted.

Per Serving: Calories: 203; Fat:6g; Protein:3g; Fiber:3g

Flourless Cream-Filled Mini Cakes
PREP: 10 MINUTES • COOK TIME: 10 MINUTES • TOTAL: 20 MINUTES • *SERVES: 8*

Ingredients
Cake:

½ cup (1 stick) unsalted butter

4 ounces unsweetened chocolate, chopped

¾ cup Swerve confectioners'-style sweetener or equivalent amount of powdered sweetener

3 large eggs

Filling:

1 (8-ounce) package cream cheese softened

¼ cup Swerve confectioners'-style sweetener

 Whipped cream

Raspberries

Instructions:

1   Preheat the Salter air fryer to 375°F. Grease eight 4-ounce ramekins. Make the cake batter: Heat the butter and chocolate in a saucepan over low heat, stirring often, until the chocolate is completely melted. Remove from the heat.
Add the sweetener and eggs and use a hand mixer on low to combine well. Set aside.
Make the cream filling: In a medium-sized bowl, mix together the cream cheese and sweetener until well combined. Taste and add more sweetener if desired. Divide the chocolate mixture among the greased ramekins, filling each one halfway. Place 1 tablespoon of the filling on top of the chocolate mixture in each ramekin.

2   Place the ramekins in the air fryer and cook for 10 minutes, or until the outside is set and the inside is soft and warm. Allow to cool completely, then top with whipped cream, if desired, and garnish with raspberries, if desired.

Chocolaty Banana Muffins

PREP: 5 MINUTES • COOK TIME: 25 MINUTES • TOTAL: 35 MINUTES • *SERVES: 12*

Ingredients

¾ cup whole wheat flour
¾ cup plain flour
¼ cup cocoa powder
¼ teaspoon baking powder
1 teaspoon baking soda
¼ teaspoon salt

2 large bananas, peeled and mashed
1 cup sugar
1/3 cup canola oil
1 egg
½ teaspoon vanilla essence
1 cup mini chocolate chips

Instructions:

1   In a large bowl, mix together flour, cocoa powder, baking powder, baking soda and salt. In another bowl, add bananas, sugar, oil, egg and vanilla extract and beat till well combined. Slowly, add flour mixture in egg mixture and mix till just combined. Fold in chocolate chips. Preheat the Salter air fryer to 345 degrees F. Grease 12 muffin molds.

2   Transfer the mixture into prepared muffin molds evenly and cook for about 20-25 minutes or till a toothpick inserted in the center comes out clean. Remove the muffin molds from Air fryer and keep on wire rack to cool for about 10 minutes. Carefully turn on a wire rack to cool completely before serving.

Halle Berries-and-Cream Cobbler

PREP: 10 MINUTES • COOK TIME: 25 MINUTES • TOTAL: 35 MINUTES • *SERVES: 4*

Ingredients

12 ounces cream cheese (1½ cups), softened
1 large egg
¾ cup Swerve confectioners'-style sweetener
½ teaspoon vanilla extract
¼ teaspoon fine sea salt
1 cup sliced fresh raspberries or strawberries
BISCUITS:
3 large egg whites
¾ cup blanched almond flour
1 teaspoon baking powder

2½ tablespoons very cold unsalted butter, cut into pieces
¼ teaspoon fine sea salt
FROSTING:
2 ounces cream cheese (¼ cup), softened
1 Tablespoon Swerve confectioners'-style sweetener or liquid sweetener
1 tablespoon unsweetened, unflavored almond milk or heavy cream
Fresh raspberries or strawberries, for garnish

Instructions:

1   Preheat the Salter air fryer to 400°F. Grease a 7-inch pie pan.
In a large mixing bowl, use a hand mixer to combine the cream cheese, egg, and sweetener until smooth. Stir in the vanilla and salt. Gently fold in the raspberries with a rubber spatula. Pour the mixture into the prepared pan and set aside. Make the biscuits: Place the egg whites in a medium-sized mixing bowl or the bowl of a stand mixer. Using a hand mixer or stand mixer, whip the egg whites until very fluffy and stiff. In a separate medium-sized bowl, combine the almond flour and baking powder. Cut in the butter and add the salt, stirring gently to keep the butter pieces intact. Gently fold the almond flour mixture into the egg whites. Use a large spoon or ice cream scooper to scoop out the dough and form it into a 2-inch-wide biscuit, making sure the butter stays in separate clumps. Place the biscuit on top of the raspberry mixture in the pan. Repeat with remaining dough to make 4 biscuits.

2   Place the pan in the air fryer and cook for 5 minutes, then lower the temperature to 325°F and bake for another 17 to 20 minutes, until the biscuits are golden brown. While the cobbler cooks, make the frosting: Place the cream cheese in a small bowl and stir to break it up. Add the sweetener and stir. Add the almond milk and stir until well combined. If you prefer a thinner frosting, add more almond milk. Remove the cobbler from the air fryer and allow to cool slightly, then drizzle with the frosting. Garnish with fresh raspberries.
Store leftovers in an airtight container in the refrigerator for up to 3 days. Reheat the cobbler in a preheated 350°F air fryer for 3 minutes, or until warmed through.

Apple Hand Pies
PREP: 5 MINUTES • COOK TIME: 8 MINUTES • TOTAL: 13 MINUTES • *SERVES: 6*

Ingredients
15-ounces no-sugar-added apple pie filling
1 store-bought crust

Instructions:

1 Lay out pie crust and slice into equal-sized squares.
   Place 2 tbsp. filling into each square and seal crust with a fork.
2 Place into the Air fryer. Cook 8 minutes at 390 degrees until golden in color.

Chocolate Meringue Cookies
PREP: 10 MINUTES PLUS 20 MINUTES TO REST • COOK TIME: 60 MINUTES • TOTAL: 1 HOUR 30 MINUTES
•*SERVES: 16 COOKIES*

Ingredients
3 large egg whites
¼ teaspoon cream of tartar

¼ cup Swerve confectioners'-style sweetener
2 tablespoons unsweetened cocoa powder

Instructions:

1. Preheat the Salter air fryer to 225°F. Line a 7-inch pie pan or a dish that will fit in your air fryer with parchment paper. In a small bowl, use a hand mixer to beat the egg whites and cream of tartar until soft peaks form. With the mixer on low, slowly sprinkle in the sweetener and mix until it's completely incorporated. Continue to beat with the mixer until stiff peaks form. Add the cocoa powder and gently fold until it's completely incorporated. Spoon the mixture into a piping bag with a ¾-inch tip. (If you don't have a piping bag, snip the corner of a large resealable plastic bag to form a ¾-inch hole.) Pipe sixteen 1-inch meringue cookies onto the lined pie pan, spacing them about ¼ inch apart.
2. Place the pan in the air fryer and cook for 1 hour, until the cookies are crispy on the outside, then turn off the air fryer and let the cookies stand in the air fryer for another 20 minutes before removing and serving.

Lemon Poppy Seed Macaroons
PREP: 10 MINUTES • COOK TIME: 14 MINUTES • TOTAL: 24 MINUTES • *SERVES: 12 COOKIES*

Ingredients
2 large egg whites, room temperature
⅓ cup Swerve confectioners'-style sweetener
2 tablespoons grated lemon zest, plus more for garnish if desired
2 teaspoons poppy seeds
1 teaspoon lemon extract

¼ teaspoon fine sea salt
2 cups unsweetened shredded coconut
LEMON ICING:
¼ cup Swerve confectioners'-style sweetener
1 tablespoon lemon juice

Instructions:

1 Preheat the Salter air fryer to 325°F. Line a 7-inch pie pan or a casserole dish that will fit inside your air fryer with parchment paper. Place the egg whites in a medium-sized bowl and use a hand mixer on high to beat the whites until stiff peaks form. Add the sweetener, lemon zest, poppy seeds, lemon extract, and salt. Mix on low until combined. Gently fold in the coconut with a rubber spatula. Use a 1-inch cookie scoop to place the cookies on the parchment, spacing them about ¼ inch apart.
2 Place the pan in the air fryer and cook for 12 to 14 minutes, until the cookies are golden and a toothpick inserted into the center comes out clean. While the cookies bake, make the lemon icing: Place the sweetener in a small bowl. Add the lemon juice and stir well. If the icing is too thin, add a little more sweetener. If the icing is too thick, add a little more lemon juice. Remove the cookies from the air fryer and allow to cool for about 10 minutes, then drizzle with the icing. Garnish with lemon zest, if desired.

Per cookie: Calories 71; Fat 7g; Protein 1g; Total carbs 3g; Fiber 2g

Blueberry Lemon Muffins
PREP: 5 MINUTES • COOK TIME: 10 MINUTES • TOTAL: 15 MINUTES • *SERVES: 12*

Ingredients

1 tsp. vanilla
Juice and zest of 1 lemon
2 eggs
1 C. blueberries

½ C. cream
¼ C. avocado oil
½ C. monk fruit
2 ½ C. almond flour

Instructions:

1   Mix monk fruit and flour together.
    In another bowl, mix vanilla, egg, lemon juice, and cream together. Add mixtures together and blend well. Spoon batter into cupcake holders.
2   Place in air fryer. Bake 10 minutes at 320 degrees, checking at 6 minutes to ensure you don't overbake them.

Per Serving: Calories: 317; Fat:11g; Protein:3g; Sugar:5g

Lemon Curd Pavlova
PREP:10 MINUTES PLUS 20 MINUTES TO REST•COOK TIME:60 MINUTES•TOTAL: 1 HOUR 30 MINUTES•*SERVES: 4*

Ingredients

SHELL:
3 large egg whites
¼ teaspoon cream of tartar
¾ cup Swerve confectioners'-style sweetener
1 teaspoon grated lemon zest
1 teaspoon lemon extract
LEMON CURD:
1 cup Swerve confectioners'-style sweetener or powdered sweetener

½ cup lemon juice
4 large eggs
½ cup coconut oil
FOR GARNISH (OPTIONAL):
Blueberries
Swerve confectioners'-style sweetener or equivalent amount of powdered sweetener

Instructions:

1   Preheat the Salter air fryer to 275°F. Thoroughly grease a 7-inch pie pan with butter or coconut oil.
    Make the shell: In a small bowl, use a hand mixer to beat the egg whites and cream of tartar until soft peaks form. With the mixer on low, slowly sprinkle in the sweetener and mix until it's completely incorporated.
    Add the lemon zest and lemon extract and continue to beat with the hand mixer until stiff peaks form.
    Spoon the mixture into the greased pie pan, then smooth it across the bottom, up the sides, and onto the rim to form a shell.
2   Cook for 1 hour, then turn off the air fryer and let the shell stand in the air fryer for 20 minutes. (The shell can be made up to 3 days ahead and stored in an airtight container in the refrigerator, if desired.)
    While the shell bakes, make the lemon curd: In a medium-sized heavy-bottomed saucepan, whisk together the sweetener, lemon juice, and eggs. Add the coconut oil and place the pan on the stovetop over medium heat. Once the oil is melted, whisk constantly until the mixture thickens and thickly coats the back of a spoon, about 10 minutes. Do not allow the mixture to come to a boil.
    Pour the lemon curd mixture through a fine-mesh strainer into a medium-sized bowl. Place the bowl inside a larger bowl filled with ice water and whisk occasionally until the curd is completely cool, about 15 minutes.
    Place the lemon curd on top of the shell and garnish with blueberries and powdered sweetener, if desired. Store leftovers in the refrigerator for up to 4 days.

Per serving: Calories 332; Fat 33g; Protein 9g; Total carbs 4g; Fiber 1g

HERITAGE OF FOOD: A FAMILY GATHERING

To survive, we need to eat. As a result, food has turned into a symbol of loving, nurturing and sharing with one another. Recording, collecting, sharing and remembering the recipes that have been passed to you by your family is a great way to immortalize and honor your family. It is these traditions that carve out your individual personality. You will not just be honoring your family tradition by cooking these recipes, but they will also inspire you to create your own variations, which you can then pass on to your children's.

The recipes are just passed on to everyone, and nobody actually possesses them. I too love sharing recipes. The collection is vibrant and rich as a number of home cooks have offered their inputs to ensure that all of us can cook delicious meals at our home. I am thankful to each one of you who has contributed to this book and has allowed their traditions to pass on and grow with others. You guys are wonderful!

I am also thankful to the cooks who have evaluated all these recipes. You're, as well as, the comments that came from your family members and friends were invaluable.

If you have the time and inclination, please consider leaving a short review wherever you can, we would love to learn more about your opinion.

https://www.amazon.com/review/review-your-purchases/

ABOUT THE AUTHOR

Elisa is a New York-based food writer, experienced chef. She loves sharing Easy, Delicious and Healthy recipes, especially the delicious and healthy meals that can be prepared using her Air fryer. Elisa is a passionate advocate for the health benefits of a low-carb lifestyle. When she's not cooking, Elisa enjoys spending time with her husband and her kids, gardening and traveling.

Printed in Great Britain
by Amazon